R.E.A.L. Leaders Wear P.I.N.K.

The Power Starters' Guide to Leadership Success

Realistic
Effective
Authentic
Leader Led

Powerful
Innovative
Natural
Knowledgeable

Dr. Donna Thomas-Rodgers
President, The Power Starters, LC

Book Cover and Interior Layout & Design by Scribe Freelance
www.scribefreelance.com

Set in Perpetua

ISBN: 978-0-615-28512-2

Printed in the United States of America

Contents

Dr. Donna's Perspective

· ❀ ·

EVERYONE HAS THE POTENTIAL to become a great leader and anyone can lead. Yes, I said *anyone* can lead. From the parent in charge of the P.T.A. to the C.E.O. of a Fortune 500 Hundred Company – we all can achieve leadership success. You see, the secret is that leaders are *made* and not *born*. I am a clear example of a manufactured leader.

My path to leadership was a fluke really. In high school I needed to take a Physical Education Class. The school had several PE options: with two left feet Dance Class was clearly out and Gymnastics was not a viable option for me either because of lack of coordination. Gym was definitely out because I did not want to mess up my hair in the middle of the day. The only option left was The United States Army's Junior Reserve Officers' Training Corps (JROTC).

JROTC was chosen because it was the path of least resistance. My original plan was to take the class for two semesters to fulfill the PE requirement. However, it was love at first sight with JROTC. I really enjoyed being in charge and leading. The downside was that, during those first couple of years I was an awful leader; a clear demonstration of how *not* to lead.

These previous good and bad experiences have allowed me further development which affords an opportunity for others to learn and grow. After years of verbally abusive comments, mistakes, and a demanding dictatorship approach to leading, I am now a R.E.A.L. leader who wears P.I.N.K.

Realistic
Effective
Authentic
Leader Led

Powerful
Innovative
Natural
Knowledgeable

You too can be a R.E.A.L. leader that wears P.I.N.K.

Realistic

The first step to PINK leadership is to be realistic.

Realistic leadership is honest leadership and it requires you to lead from three areas: your head, your heart, and your gut.

> *Your Head — Tells you what to do*
> *Your Heart — Keeps you human*
> *Your Gut — Keeps you safe*

When you stay in tuned to these three areas, you <u>will</u> be effective.

Embrace Change

Our inability to change impacts our ability to succeed

THE GREATEST CHALLENGE TO CHANGE is fear. We don't know what the change will bring and, as a result, we often fear the unknown. When you decide that you are not going to change then you become stagnant and you will stop growing. You have told yourself that this is as good as it gets.

When you change your mindset and embrace changes as they occur, you open your life up to new possibilities.

Here is an example:
Talking first and listening second was my thought process. When engaged in conversations, I would just stand there waiting to respond as the dialogue was more of a debate than a conversation. The end result was that people no longer wanted to talk to me because it was too challenging. Finally, someone was brave enough to tell me about the awful habit. Initially, hearing about my ineffective listening behavior caused me to become defensive and reject the feedback.

After going home and really thinking about the person's feedback, it was true there was a flaw that existed in me. The next day my intent was to become an effective listener. As a result, everyone in the office was given my permission to tell me every time that I was not demonstrating good listening skills. With the help of my peers and my team my listening skills have improved.

Change is an integral process in the leadership journey. The growth and development that is derived from change is well worth the trip. Be willing to let go and embrace change every opportunity that you are faced with it. PINK leaders are willing to change any habit that will increase their ability to lead successfully.

Here is an exercise that will assist you in your change efforts.

Exercise:
Write down three major changes that you need to make as a leader. Next, write down how you will implement those changes and when the results of those changes should be visible. Finally, commit to the changes.

You will also need to hold yourself accountable to the changes so that they stick. There needs to be a harsh repercussion if you do not adhere to the changes that you have decided to make. This is the only way you will ensure that you will commit to the change.

Changes:
1.
2.
3.

Tactics to implement:

1.

2.

3.

Visible results of the change (insert a date):

1.

2.

3.

To achieve success, you will need to make some changes. After all, nothing ever changes if nothing ever changes.

Be Coachable

In order to be coached you need to be coachable

AT 17 YEARS OLD THERE WAS NOTHING that anyone could tell me about running track so there was no need to listen to the track coach. Prior to running high school track, I had won most of my neighborhood races which enabled me to become the local star on my block. The track coach was cramping my style with all of her nonsense about technique and form.

Here is what occurred:

The first day of practice the track coach informed me that sprinters needed to start their races using starting blocks. Because not using blocks had worked for me in the past, there was no need to fix what was not broken. The indoor track season began without me using the starting blocks. Each race, everyone else used the starting blocks and they would beat me out of the start. My methodology was flawed it took twice as much energy to catch up with the rest of the runners during the race. Not using the staring blocks was ineffective and the result was never placing or winning a race. So much for being the neighborhood champion.

While continuing to lose races, I still refused to use the starting blocks. Finally, after two months my coach demanded that everyone use the starting blocks. Fury set in my bones at the thought of learning how to set the blocks up and push off with my feet. It was difficult for me to make it to a standing running position coming out of the blocks. The process created internal frustration and the feeling of giving up was constantly a lingering thought in my mind.

One day during practice, with some reservation, I explained to the coach the difficulty coming out of the blocks and standing to run was creating for me. The coach helped and finally the purpose of using the starting blocks became clear to me. She continued to work with me until I was able to master the task.

After receiving the one-with-one coaching and applying the coach's knowledge I benefited from her expertise and actually started winning races. It was a defining moment for me. She was able to help me only when I was willing to receive the coaching.

There are three key factors to being coachable:

1. *Submitting to the expert.*
2. *The willingness to listen.*
3. *Application of the information.*

The lesson learned from my track experience in high school still applies today. Using my head I know that to be coached you have to be a willing participant.

Solicit Feedback

❧

Feedback is the gift that keeps on giving

IN THE PAST, I DID NOT LIKE to ask for feedback on my performance or my leadership skills. It is amazing but, for some reason it felt as though the feedback would always be negative. Fortunately for me a mentor explained how the feedback process actually works and the benefits of it.

Feedback, when it is given correctly, is meant to develop your skills. As a result, everyone is allowed to provide performance focused feedback – family, friends, peers, employees, superiors and clients. Their information, for the most part, has proven to be invaluable. By taking the advice of the mentor feedback is now a part of my leadership development.

Here are some tips as you receive feedback:
A REAL PINK Leader will tell you that when you are receiving the feedback to listen with an attentive ear and filter the information. While you are receiving the feedback, write it down and review it a couple of days later. Think PINK by conducting self analysis and if it truly is going to help you, then apply it; if you are not going to benefit from it, do not use it.

Here is an example of me asking for and then applying feedback:

During team member one-with-one sessions, I would have to ask how they felt about my performance. There was one team member who informed me that after asking them to perform a task, I never said "thank you." Her words lingered in my office after we completed the one-with-one. After reviewing previous encounters with my other team members, she was correct. My "thank you's" were sporadic at best.

Immediately the behavior was changed and it has been a tremendous asset to my leadership skills. Today "thank you" is an integral part of my leadership skills. That experience has taught me that the little things mean just as much as the large ones. Every completed request deserves a thank you. PINK leaders use the term often and mean it with all sincerity.

Begin to solicit feedback – you will benefit a great deal.

Exercise:
Here is a proven method to be successful when receiving feedback. Ask the following questions:

1. *What role does this person play in the situation?*
2. *Are they really focused on my development?*
3. *Do they like me? Are they friend or foe?*
4. *How will they benefit from giving me the information?*

5. *Do I trust and value their suggestions?*
6. *Are they credible?*

Once the questions have been answered make an informed decision about their feedback then determine whether to use it or lose it.

Feedback is a gift. I have taken feedback and leveraged it throughout my career. My soldiers and employees have been the direct beneficiaries of it.

Eliminate the Clutter in Your Life

❊

Mess creates stress

WHEN YOU HAVE A LIFE THAT IS FILLED with clutter, it is impossible to be organized and see things clearly. To eliminate the clutter in your life, you need to do an overhaul at least twice a year and a minor clean up every quarter. This applies to all areas in your life – office, home, car, and garage as well.

Here is a look at the clutter process:

We have a tendency to tell ourselves that we will one day get back into the suit so we store it. We believe that we may need a particular file later so we store it. We believe that we will finish building the table for the deck so we store the supplies for it in the garage. Years pass and we end up with a plethora of clothes, files, tools and supplies that we will never use – but, we keep them "just in case we need them."

The fact of the matter is that we don't want to let go. Holding on to all of that clutter provides a false sense of security in our lives. Realistically speaking, you cannot move forward successfully if you are still holding on to the past.

Here is a process to eliminate the clutter in your life:

Closet – In your closet if you have not worn the item in the last year, give it away. If you have multiple sizes pick a size, stick with it, and give every other size away.

Garage – This is not a large storage bin for your clutter. If you cannot park in your garage, have a garage sale and then donate everything that is not sold. Then park your car(s) in the garage.

Office – In your office find out how many years you need to keep records for an audit and then shred, recycle and donate everything else. People should see you when they walk into your office, not mounds of paper, files and clutter. Also, if possible, store the files electronically. Hard copies can easily be converted to electronic copies with the use of a scanner. This will reduce your storage space immensely. Cleaning your office will also enable you to focus on going green and reduce your carbon foot print.

Car – Finally the car; It is a means of transportation, not a mobile storage bin. The only items that you need in your vehicle are an emergency kit in the trunk and an umbrella. Everything else is just excess junk.

Once you have removed the clutter, conduct quarterly audits to ensure that you are not falling back into old hoarding habits. Then twice a year conduct your overhaul and donate any item that has not been used during its season. Remember the old saying: "one man's trash is another man's treasure." Let someone else treasure your clutter.

Get Organized and Stay Organized

❈

You can't remember everything all of the time, so write it down

IN MY YOUTH THERE WAS NEVER A need to write anything down because I only had a couple of tasks to complete each day it was simple to remember them. As an officer in the military this process did not work – there were too many people, too much equipment, and too many lives at stake. Becoming organized was the ultimate key to my success.

There were several options – planners but they were too bulky for me, writing the tasks on a calendar but it could be misplaced; the final option was a to-do-list. This method was the most effective for me. Since that time a calendar has been added through e-mail. The list and the calendar keep me in line causing me to rarely miss an event, appointment, conference call, or deadline.

A successful life stems well beyond your profession. Your entire life needs to be organized. When every aspect of your life is in order, you can focus on accomplishing goals. Being organized will enable you to live a full, balanced life at the office and at home. You owe it to yourself and your family to get organized and stay organized.

Exercise:

Develop a system that will start you on your path to becoming organized. The most effective method is to begin with the Franklin Covey Planners, or electronic planners, most cell phones have calendars as well. They will help you stay on track. I also recommend leveraging your e-mail calendar as it will automatically remind you of meetings and appointments. You can also review it daily, weekly and monthly.

You will also need to set aside time daily to review your next day's activities. This will enable you to be well prepared for the events that you will need to attend. The essential key to becoming organized and staying organized is to commit to it, knowing that your ultimate success lies in your ability to stay organized.

It takes at least 21 days to form a habit. Commit to the process for at least three weeks. At that point it will become a habit and become apart of your daily leadership activities.

You will remain organized by consistently checking on your status. You have to consistently hold yourself accountable. Your head and your gut will tell you what to do. Your head will let you know internally when you are straying away from the regime. Your gut will also put you back on track as soon as you recognize that you are swaying. When you get and stay organized, your life stays on track.

Eliminate Distractions

The quickest way to miss success is by becoming distracted

DISTRACTIONS EXIST FOR THE SOLE purpose of taking you off of your success glide path. When you focus on them, you weaken your ability to succeed. The first step to eliminating distractions is to recognize them when they occur.

There are a million distractions that occur on any given day. They disguise themselves as problems, fires, hot topics, gossip, emergencies, etc. When something happens that is not directly related to the task at hand, I listen to my gut and fix it immediately and then return to what is important. The less time spent on distractions, the more time there is to focus on becoming successful.

This is what typically happens when we are working diligently and a distraction occurs. We stop what we are doing, start working on the distraction and then we return to our task/project. The problem is that often we are no longer "in the mood" to work on it. We then make excuses — as to why it is okay to begin to slack. It is never okay to slack because you have been distracted. Clearly, you should enjoy your life. Just prioritize what is important and put most of your efforts to that end.

Here is an example to further demonstrate my point: While working on this book two e-mail notifications appeared on the screen. The first e-mail was from a friend from high school who wanted me to fill out a quiz. Once it was completed it needed to be returned to the person that sent it and everyone else on the distribution list. After reviewing the list very quickly this was not a productive task. There would be no benefit to me, other than people would know that I had grown from high school.

After reviewing the second e-mail of a blog that someone sent to me. He wanted me to respond to it, but I did not. In less than two minutes I determined that neither e-mail warranted me to stop writing and respond immediately.

Those were simple examples, but you understand the intent. Responding to either of those e-mails would have caused me to become distracted. Once I finished the e-mails then I could have potentially gone on to something else and may have never taken the time to complete this book. Please do not misunderstand the point you need to respond to e-mails. However, if it is your designated time to work on what is going to give you the success you deserve, then nothing should interfere with that time. Later in the week the quiz was completed and a response was given to the blog.

PINK Leaders are able to discern when something is a distraction because of their ability to remain focused. REAL Leaders are able to eliminate the distraction quickly staying focused on building and sustaining success.

Take a Risk

Taking a risk is not the same as being risky

IT WAS THE HEIGHT OF MY MILITARY career when my resignation was submitted. No one in the military could understand why. They told me all of these terrible stories about being a civilian, indicating how much of a challenge it would be for someone as rigid as me. I sort of listened and then decided to do what I felt was best for my life and the future of my own career.

With some resistance and a little fear, I resigned my commission and left the military. Taking a ten thousand dollar pay cut my career as a civilian began as a front line manager with a large snack food company. The position required me to move to Orlando, Florida.

A big risk was taken in October 2000 and it was well worth it. I have shaped the lives of hundreds of people by setting out to change my own. By deciding to leave my comfort zone, people are now living their dreams. Sure, there have been challenges along the way, but it has been a rewarding experience. Nothing feels better than to hear success stories from those that have benefited from your leadership.

Exercise:

Identify one area in your life in which you have been playing it safe in and do a "180." Take a risk. Watch what a difference it will make in your life. I am not suggesting to throw away all that you have accomplished, simply let go and grow, so that you can accomplish more. Examples are: start your own business, write a book, travel more frequently, start speaking publicly, or pursue your lifelong dream.

Taking a risk does not mean living a risky life. Take a chance even if you are afraid, you will be glad that you did. REAL leaders take calculated risks that everyone can benefit from.

Go For It

*Going for it means living your life with no regrets,
no doubts, and no fears*

THE PERSON THAT HINDERS YOUR success the most is YOU. Yes, I said it. You are the only person that can stop your success. No one else can stop you from achieving your dreams. Others may try but, if and when you stop, it is the result of a choice that you have made.

Of course, we would like to blame our inability to achieve success on circumstances. If we really took the time to understand why we hesitate or never go after our dreams, it is because of ourselves. It has everything to do with us and nothing to do with anyone else. We believe that somehow if we go for it and we fail then it was all for naught. Whenever you are in pursuit of a goal or a dream it will never be in vain. Sure there is great fear, and I understand your apprehension. It is okay to feel the fear — it is not okay to submit to it.

There is not one person who has achieved success that has not experienced set backs, fears, or failures. Do not let any of those things stop you from pursuing success. YOU control YOUR life. Listen to your gut, stop making excuses and begin to "Go for it." Whatever it is, you only have one life. Live it to the fullest and pursue your dreams.

PINK Leaders go for it, and have lives that are fulfilled and successful.

Believe in Yourself

When we believe in ourselves we can conquer the world

I CAN ACCOMPLISH ANYTHING. ONE of the only reasons that I am still standing is because of my strong sense of belief in my own abilities. By developing a strong relationship with myself, I became my number one fan. Knowing that no matter what occurs in my life I will be there to support me.

The strongest belief in oneself often comes when times are toughest, or when facing a difficult obstacle. We have all been there. We believe that we can accomplish a goal and then something negative happens and it causes us to doubt our capabilities. We then begin to question everything around us. We become confused and afraid and then we are paralyzed from the fear. We instantly feel as though we cannot accomplish even the simplest task, like crossing the street. Because of the doubt and fear we no longer believe in ourselves. Then we have no idea how to proceed.

Because tumultuous times will occur on your path to achieve success you will need to develop a significant relationship with yourself. The primary reason for this relationship is that there may not be anyone else around to encourage you. When you are one with yourself the strength to press forward comes from inside of you.

Having a strong sense of self will enable you to persevere until you have achieved your goals. As a result, you will need to be able to listen instinctively to your gut and then to your head during those trials and tribulations.

Exercise:
Your greatest cheerleader can be yourself. You spend more time with yourself than anyone else does. So start from there. You must wake up each day and tell yourself how great you are. Tell yourself that anything you set out to accomplish will work. You have to give yourself hugs, and look in the mirror, smile, and say "I love you; you mean the world to me." "You are a winner." "You can do it."

The greatest reward to hard work and determination is success. The power of being PINK begins and ends with you believing in yourself.

Effective

What is effective leadership? We often hear "He or she is effective," and we feel as though they have a talent that most don't possess.

Conversely, we hear, "They were not an effective leader" and we believe that they are flawed in some way.

In a nut shell, effective leadership is equated to winning, and achieving goals. Ineffective leadership translates into failure.

I have been effective and ineffective throughout my leadership career. During the ineffective moments I revaluated the situation and worked through how things could have been handled differently. The purpose of the review was to ensure that I would not model those ineffective behaviors again.

The truth is that as leaders, even when we strive to be effective, we could miss the mark for reasons outside of our control. The goal in effective leadership is to become well equipped so that you minimize/eliminate your ineffective moments. This section will explore how you can consistently focus on becoming effective.

It starts with setting high standards.

Set High Standards

Success will never be achieved with mediocre standards

MOST PEOPLE WILL MEET WHATEVER minimum standard is set for them. For example, in school if "C" is passing then most students will work on passing classes with "C's". In fact, they are excited when they receive a "B." I was a part of the average group and am a perfect example of meeting a standard.

When I was in school working toward my bachelor's degree, I needed to maintain a 2.5 GPA to keep my scholarship. The first two years my GPA was 2.75. This GPA was above the minimum standard and was close to a "B- average" – it was good performance. Things were going along well and then it happened. During my junior year the Graduate Advisor said that a 3.0 GPA was necessary to apply to law school.

Reality set in and the vacation was over. I really had to apply myself by earning "A's" to improve my GPA. The next two semesters were spent working to increase my grades. By the first semester of my senior year my goal had been accomplished. My diligent efforts proved to be a success, graduating with a 3.02 GPA, making the Dean's list, and acceptance into Howard's Law School. After graduating I decided to go into the Army instead of attending law school.

A couple of years later I started graduate school while in the Army. The standards to stay in graduate school were more challenging than in undergrad. You could only receive two "C's" during the entire program. My friend earned two "C's" with the first courses that she took. The Dean of our program kindly asked her to leave. He informed her that she did not have what it took to complete the program. His exact words were, "she lacked focus and commitment." With a new mindset change from the undergrad years there was a greater sense of focus. Being a Commissioned Officer was a significant contributing factor as well. A higher minimum standard equated to higher performance and upon graduation the result was a 3.8 GPA.

Post graduate school was difficult to say the least. The only possible grades were "A", "B" and "I" (incomplete). During the program we had to complete 66 credit hours and the dissertation process which consisted of three phases and live research. The program also had a time restriction of five years. The minimum standards were the most challenging I had experienced in my academic career. The program was completed in four years with a 3.95 GPA.

The minimum standards set did not require me to perform at a higher level in undergrad. Those post graduate years' minimum standards were more like maximum standards. The stringent minimum's required me to push myself to new levels. To be honest, I really did not know that I was capable of performing at those levels until I was pushed. When the minimum standards were raised I performed at the next level expected.

PINK leaders push themselves to higher levels and then set new levels to achieve. If you want to be successful then get ready to live up to and exceed high standards. If the standards are too low for you then make your own. This is what we opted to do in the Army.

We had to take a physical fitness test twice a year. There were three areas that were graded: push-ups, sit-ups, and a two mile run. Each event was timed. We received two minutes to complete sit-ups and push-ups then we ran two miles. There were standards for each event that were broken down into age groups. The highest score possible to achieve was 300 points.

The average score that most soldiers received was 210 points. There were, however, soldiers that were able to max out the requirements in each event. They always scored a perfect score of 300 points. Most times they would give minimal effort and still achieve the maximum score. In order to push them to their next level of fitness the Army developed the extended scale. The max score went from 300 to 400 points. This enabled the standards to be increased and soldiers were challenged again to excel.

The point of interest was that the extended scale encouraged soldiers that were not scoring 300 to work towards increasing their scores. We saw a drastic increase as a direct result of the extended scoring scale from all soldiers. This is another clear illustration that we are capable of achieving greater results when more is asked of us. Most often we just need to be pushed to achieve a new level of success.

Exercise:

1. *Identify an area in your organization in which you need to raise the bar.*
2. *Identify team members or managers that need to have their performance standards raised.*

Develop S.M.A.R.T. (Specified, Measurable, Attainable, Realistic and Timely) action plans to work towards meeting the new standards. You will need to set interim goals along the way to measure performance. An interim goal is a smaller goal that will roll up into the larger goal. It is a check and balance to ensure that you will achieve your ultimate goal.

Here is an example of a S.M.A.R.T action plan that was developed in the first week of quarter one.

Acquire 20 new corporate clients by the end of quarter four. This new client base will generate $25,000 dollars of new business with $12,500 in residual income over the next year.

The interim goal will be that each quarter the need to obtain five new corporate clients, which equates to less than 2 clients a month. Each month determine if the interim goal is being achieved. Reviewing the strategy monthly will ensure that the quarter four goal of 20 new corporate clients is met.

The process of setting high standards and checking on their progress means that you are operating in a PINK capacity and consistently will ensure that you and your organization are effective.

Go For the Gold

❖

There is no half stepping when you are focused
on winning the championship

ANYONE THAT HAS WON A CHAMPIONSHIP has worked very hard to achieve success. The Olympics, in my opinion, is the epitome of championship competition. It is the best of the best from all over the world competing. What is even greater is that all of the participants share one common goal, winning a gold medal.

They spend years working on every aspect of their craft to ensure they will win the gold. They lift weights, they eat properly, and they practice for hours, several times a day. They make the necessary sacrifices to ensure that they will be victorious. Think about it, Olympic competitors train to win the gold. You will never hear them say, "I only want to win a bronze medal." Their only objective is to go for the gold.

To become effective you need to strive for your own gold medal in your profession. Complete the exercise below. It is your plan to win a championship.

Exercise:
Write down what equates to winning a gold medal in
your field/industry. Then write down a detailed plan
that you will execute to achieve the medal. When you

have achieved your goal ensure that you reward yourself and celebrate your win. Continue this process throughout your career and you will consistently be effective and successful.

The Goal:

_____

_____

_____

_____

_____

The Plan:

_____

_____

_____

_____

_____

PINK leaders are focused on being the best, they know that they will be successful. Go for the gold because that is what champions do.

Be a Thermostat, Not a Thermometer

Set the temperature, don't take it

EFFECTIVE LEADERS CONTROL THEIR destiny. They do not sit idle and wonder why things are occurring. They take control of the situation and become responsible for the outcome.

My second job was at a fast food restaurant. The schedule that was given to me was awful. The primary task was always the front cashier. It was boring after the morning rush and my day seemed to drone on forever. I worked there with two of my cousins. They both wanted to try something new as well. They however, just complained about favoritism and that it was not fair how we were being treated. They were demonstrating thermometer behavior.

Conversely, my approach was that of a thermostat. One day when counting my drawer down with my supervisor, I simply asked why he always scheduled me as the front cashier. He explained that he needed someone fast during the rush hours and my performance met those needs. My response to him was that after the morning rush there was really no more work for me to complete. The lulls in my day needed to be filled with other tasks. He thought about it and said, "okay, what else would you like to do?" I wanted to work the drive-thru and work on the grill. When he told me that it would be too much, my response was "I can handle it." He agreed and we set up my new assignment for the next work week.

The next week the new tasks began. I was able to handle all three tasks and began to make salads as well. Being crossed trained in three additional tasks increased my marketability. My schedule and assigned tasks were controlled by me. Setting the tone for the work day was a clear demonstration of thermostat behavior.

Exercise:

1. *In what area in your organization are you demonstrating thermometer behavior?*

_____

_____

_____

_____

_____

2. *Write down action plans to turn your situation around and become a thermostat?*

_____

_____

_____

_____

_____

_____

_____

_____

In life you have two options, you can sit around and complain like my cousins, or you can change your fate, like I did.

A thermometer takes the temperature. A thermostat sets the temperature.

Develop a Strong, Sustainable Network

Your network is the life line to success; establishing a strong support system enables you to prevail

WITHOUT MY CONSTANT NURTURING AND developing of my network my level of success would be minuscule. I have maintained contact with fellow soldiers, colleagues in Corporate America, teachers, doctors, attorneys, childhood friends, radio personalities, law enforcement officers, and the list goes on. We have developed a true partnership and friendship and we can depend on one another. It does not matter what industry or field you operate in, you will need access to people from all walks of life.

Exercise:
The first step to building a network is "small talk". Wherever you go, talk to people to find out who they are and what commonalities you share. Have coffee and lunch with them and just get to know them as a person. Exchange information and then follow up with them periodically just to check-in. The relationship will begin to grow and as long as you consistently maintain contact they will remain a constant in your network.

Being successful will require you to have the ability to establish effective, sustainable relationships.

Stay Focused

You can't drive forward looking through the rear view mirror; focus on where you are going, not where you have been

HAVE YOU EVER DECIDED THAT YOU were going to work towards a goal and then all hell breaks loose? Before you decided to excel, life was simple. No adversity, no issues, no problems – your life was a well oiled machine. This was the reason you decided to move forward. Here is another secret, when you are growing and working on becoming better, things will happen because you are moving forward. It is as if you are swimming upstream. When you are breaking away from your normal routine, obstacles will occur. You will need to remain focused, however, to ensure that you accomplish your goal.

Here is an example of a sequence of events that transpired while working on my doctorate. During those years there were many tumultuous set-backs and adversities. There was the divorce, my daughter had just turned one, about $60,000 in debt and my nearest family member 965 miles away. Loneliness ensued and the grief process began. There was a need for a positive distraction from all the agony, the experience from the divorce and becoming a single parent had brought. It was the perfect time to go back to school and work on my doctorate.

About 18 months into the program I had to move back home to sell my house to pay off the debt. The move from sunny Orlando, Florida back to Detroit, Michigan was not an easy decision to make having not lived in the north in 10 years. Moving back home significantly altered my life. One of the changes was transitioning from working first shift in Orlando to working second shift in Detroit. Additionally, the rest of the program would need to be completed in Detroit which consisted of 35 credits and finishing the Dissertation.

The move was devastating for me. It really was a setback and it felt like failure for me with the transition from living in my own home to living in a room in my parent's home. It was a difficult time. The focus was on the end state which was to finish school and eliminate the divorce debt.

About 18 months after moving home, we left my parents home and moved into an apartment. A couple months after moving into the apartment I had an outpatient surgery that almost killed me. As a result of the surgery, it was back to live with my parents during my recovery. The surgery halted everything – no walking, no working, and completing my dissertation was virtually impossible. Once again my progress was stifled and thoughts of giving up entered my mind.

After four years the course work and the dissertation were completed even with multiple setbacks. Remaining focused throughout those years has provided more options for me and my daughter. Also never wanting to sell another house, move back home or pay large debts were motivating factors as well. Although there were many moments during those four years that I could have quit, in the end my goals were accomplished.

In life there are going to be difficult moments. They are simply moments, and time is going to pass whether we do nothing or something. Set a goal, stay focused and accomplish it. You win when you persevere and it feels great when you succeed.

Finish What You Start

⁂

The best projects are those that you complete

DO YOU KNOW SOMEONE THAT IS always working on something and they never really complete anything? I am sure that we all do and if you don't, then maybe you are the person that never completes anything. Success is all about goal setting and completion. A successful glide path is one that can be measured over time. If you are constantly starting and stopping, then there will be nothing to measure your success. You can only achieve success when you have established a strong system of completing what you start.

Here is an example:
I had a friend – we will call her Kathy. She was always starting a new Job or project and never finishing it. She decided that she was going to go into the catering business. She was passionate about cooking and she was very good at it. We all believed that she would succeed because she enjoyed preparing elegant meals. She located a building for office space with a kitchen then she hired a staff. She had several clients lined up and the she began to cater events. Six months into the process the company was not profiting at the rate that Kathy projected and Kathy became afraid. She followed her fears of past

failures and she closed the business. A month later she was downtrodden as she went back to her corporate job and she was miserable. She hated the job but it was safe and a steady income so she stayed in her position.

Closing the business should not have been her first and only option. She should have analyzed exactly where the gap in profits were coming from. She then should have established a game plan to eliminate the gap within a realistic, defined time line. This was the missing link in establishing a strong foundation of finishing what she had started.

Also, if she had an effective support system/network, she would have been able to leverage them. She could have consorted with other catering businesses to mentor her and establish a developmental plan with her. Finally, she could have at least stayed the course to turn the business around and begin to generate profitable growth. By giving up too soon she has not learned the skills that are required to run a successful start-up business. Staying the course would have given her the tools needed to achieve success in business and personal capacities.

When you finish what you start you will grow and develop new skills. Even if it is as simple as putting a jigsaw puzzle together, successful leaders figure out how to make it through any challenge. They understand that the finish line is always the goal. Anything short of that does not equate to success.

Do it Today, Procrastination is the Enemy

There is only one thing gained
from procrastination...nothing

I LIKE TO REFER TO PROCRASTINATION AS a thief that comes to rob you of your ability to achieve your destiny. The main reason that you procrastinate is because you don't enjoy what needs to be done. If given the choice you would rather not do it. When you are putting things off you need to understand that at some point the task will need to be completed.

When the time arrives to finish the task, it brings a high level of stress along with it. The moment that you have to face the task it appears as King Kong towering over you. It is in that moment that you wished you would have not waited but by then it is too late. Then you rush to finish, knowing full well that it is not your best effort.

When you make a conscious decision to delay completing the task, you have killed your ability to be successful. You have allowed the thief to come in and steal your ability to accomplish tasks in a timely manner. You inhibit your ability to move on to the next task.

If procrastination were a good thing, there would be awards for it. I guarantee that you will never hear about someone winning a prestigious award for neglecting their responsibilities. It is never acceptable to put off any task when you are focused on being successful. You have to ensure that you complete everything on time consistently. So say goodbye to the thief and say hello to no more procrastination and grief.

Here is what needs to take place. Your new mantra to every task is "DO IT NOW" while you have the time, the energy and can give it 100% of your effort. Many successful leaders have to frequently complete tasks that they loath. They complete the task anyway because they understand that procrastination is the enemy. No one ever said that it would be easy. One thing is for certain, it does not get any easier when you put it off.

So again…

DO IT NOW

Handle Conflict When it Occurs

The worst conflict is one that goes unresolved

IF YOU LIKE CONFLICT, RAISE YOUR HAND. Most of us would live a full life and be okay if we never had to incur conflict. This, however, is not likely. Personally, I hate conflict. However, what I hate even more is avoiding conflict. It takes great effort to confront conflict, but it is necessary to achieve success.

When leaders avoid conflict it is like a disease that festers and, slowly but surely, affects the entire organization. We all have our preferred method of handling conflict but, depending on the situation, you will need to have other tactics to resolve conflicts.

Effective leadership will require you to have multiple processes that you can leverage to address conflict. Effective leadership will mean that you have to intervene when conflict occurs. You will need to eliminate it as quickly as it surfaces. As a result, there are several methods that you can use in regards to situations of conflict.

You have several options when confronted with conflict:

Run

Avoid it
Walk away
Stand firm and lash out
Compromise
Collaborate

The most effective method is to collaborate. When you collaborate you are striving for win/win — both sides will be happy with the outcome. The challenge is in finding out the root cause of the conflict and then establishing a solution that resolves the conflict.

Here is an example:
We had a new automated system installed in the warehouse. Most of the team members grew to like the system after a couple of weeks of its implementation. There was one tenured team member — we will call him Bob — who would constantly manually override the system. His manual overrides would cause everyone on the team to have to wait on him to bring product to the order picking lanes. This became a source of conflict for the team members.

Bob was okay to deal with until he was told that he was not performing well in his daily job functions. No one wanted to talk to him about his misuse of the system because he could be confrontational. The team just avoided talking to him. At the end of the night, the floor supervisor would end up staying over after the shift ended to audit the warehouse. This caused even more conflict. After several weeks the issue was brought to my attention.

Immediately we sat down with Bob. After listening to both sides of the situation, I found out Bob did not understand how the system operated. The floor supervisor retrained him and the problem was resolved.

There were two choices in that situation:

1. Let the floor supervisor stay late and audit the warehouse, which was impacting overtime and his work/life balance.
2. Confront the situation and collaborate to resolve the issue.

When REAL leaders are faced with conflict, they collaborate – everyone wins.

Go Above and Beyond

❁

The sky has no limits and neither should you

TO CELEBRATE MY AUNT'S 65TH BIRTHDAY we went to lunch and shopping. While we drove she reviewed a copy of my dissertation and she told me how proud she was of my accomplishment. She went on tell me that I had accomplished more than her and my uncle could have ever imagined. Her comment did not sit well with me. Once we finished shopping and eating, we drove back to house. After giving her a hug she walked into her house. Her words were still lingering, "I had accomplished more than they had imagined…"

During the drive home the words resonated in my ears and they just did not make me feel good. She told me that I had accomplished more than she and my uncle (her brother not her husband) could have ever imagined. It was good that she waited to tell me her thoughts as an adult having earned three degrees. The words could have potentially limited my success if she had told me her opinion in my youth.

Her intent was to give me a compliment, but it came across as an insult. I never thought that I would only go to college and get a job. There are no limits to my abilities. Of course I was going to go above and beyond her expectations; my life was destined to go beyond what she thought about my capabilities. The lesson learned that day was that I own my success and no one else. PINK leaders never let someone else place boundaries on their success.

As a PINK leader your success is not determined by what anyone else believes that you are capable of becoming. It is solely up to you. You can go well beyond their expectations. There truly are no limits to what you can accomplish in life. The only limits we have are the ones that we place on ourselves. The sky has no limits and neither should you!

Authentic

Authentic leadership entails being genuine and honest. Leaders have to take the hard right over the easy wrong and never compromise their belief system or their integrity to achieve a goal or to win.

REAL Leadership success will come to you and it will be sustainable when you operate with authenticity.

Honesty is the Best Policy

❋

Honesty begins and ends with you

I HAVE WORKED WITH A LOT OF LEADERS that talked a good game. They were great salesmen. They were terrible leaders. Great leaders are great because they are clear and honest about who they are and where they are taking their teams. Your leadership success starts with you being honest.

Being honest encompasses understanding who you are and what you will need to do to achieve success. Honesty is more than telling the truth and having a strong character of integrity. REAL leader honesty will require self analysis. You will need to begin and continue to take stock of your leadership skills. This review will enable you to focus on specific areas to achieve well rounded success.

Exercise:
Here are some questions that you need to answer with regards to where you are currently.

What is your greatest strength?

_____

_____

_____

_____

_____

_____

_____

What is your greatest weakness?

_____

_____

_____

_____

_____

_____

_____

What area do you need the most focus?

_____

_____

_____

_____

_____

_____

_____

What will you need to eliminate to achieve success?

_____

_____

_____

_____

_____

_____

_____

What will you need to start to achieve success?

_____

_____

_____

_____

_____

_____

_____

What will you need to continue to achieve success?

_____

_____

_____

_____

_____

_____

_____

REAL leadership is honest leadership.

Treat People With Dignity and Respect

People will follow you everywhere when they respect you

IT IS EASY TO WORK WITH SOMEONE THAT you respect. You will no doubt achieve outstanding results. Conversely, it's when you don't feel valued and appreciated that your performance will suffer. PINK leaders consistently treat their teams with dignity and respect. They understand that when people are treated poorly they become resentful and disengaged. The most important aspects to understand about delivering dignity and respect are that it occurs over time and it must be authentic.

If you find that you are having difficulties giving or earning respect then you need to sit down with the person/team and find out why. Once you have identified the reason, work towards resolving the problem. Then you can move forward with a relationship that will foster respect and growth to achieve your goals.

Exercise:

1. *Have a meeting with your team and ask for open and honest feedback on how they feel they are being treated. Take notes during the meeting.*

2. *If you know that having a meeting with the entire team will not give you the information that you need, then meet with them individually during one-with-ones and find out how they feel they are treated by you.*

3. *Once you have talked with your team, review the notes and adjust your behavior accordingly, if needed.*

The purpose of the exercise is to receive feedback on your culture's climate and make any necessary corrections. Your objective is to foster an environment where all team members feel that they are treated with dignity and respect; because people that feel valued add value.

Look People in the Eye When You Talk to Them

I never trusted a man whose eyes I could not see

EYE CONTACT IS VERY IMPORTANT IN authentic leadership. Think about the President of the United States. What if he gave the State of the Union Address looking down at the podium for the entire speech? We would all begin to question his ability to lead our country effectively. If you fail to look your team in the eye they will question your creditability as their leader.

Always look the person you are talking to in the eye. When speaking in front of a group, do not just scan across the whole group. In public speaking, this is known as 'windshield wiper eye movement'. Rather, choose one person to make eye contact with first, hold the eye contact until the completion of your sentence or your point, then choose someone else to make eye contact with.

Exercise:
If you have difficulty looking others in the eye while speaking, practice by talking to yourself in the mirror. Ensure that you maintain eye contact with yourself at all times.

Once you are confident doing this, begin to perform this task with your loved ones. Tell them this is a challenge for you and you need them to provide feedback when you are speaking. Tell them to praise you when you actually look at them while speaking. This will give you positive reinforcement. You will then naturally become comfortable speaking to people while simultaneously looking them in their eyes. This will increase your confidence and, in turn, increase your competence. When you are able to articulate your thoughts verbally and present them in a confident manner, everyone will be interested in what you are saying

REAL Leaders are never afraid to look into the eyes of those that they lead.

Empower Your Team / Employees / Subordinates

* ✖ *

Develop others to enable them to meet their potential

THE BEST GIFT THAT YOU CAN GIVE ANY employee, team, or peer is empowerment. When people feel empowered they can climb the highest mountain and swim the widest sea. I have found that along the journey to empower others you grow as well. The energy that an empowered employee possesses is magnificent.

It feels good as a leader to know that someone has achieved greatness because of the empowering skills that you have given to them. My heart is warmed when someone tells me that they did not think that it was possible but, because of my words or actions, they were able to complete their goals.

I have had the opportunity to empower people. My soldiers have finished their degrees and completed Officer Candidate School, transitioning from being enlisted soldiers to Commissioned Officers. Several of my team members were promoted into management and achieved great leadership success.

Authentic leadership is about using your head and your heart to inspire others to meet their potential. When this transpires we all win.

Exercise:

Identify at least one action plan for everyone on your team to work on where they will be empowered. It can be as simple as facilitating a meeting or as complex as developing the next business strategy. Document the action plan during their one-with-ones and track it to completion. Once the goals have been obtained, celebrate the win.

Transfer the power to your team and watch them explode into greatness.

Establish Trust and be Trustworthy

❖

The hardest leadership trait to establish is trust. It is also the easiest to lose. When you earn it, treasure it.

ARE YOU WILLING TO WORK HARD FOR someone that you cannot trust? When you do not trust someone you will never put your best effort forward. Most people will always hold something back "just in case" something goes wrong. I will be the first to admit that it is impossible for me to work with someone that I do not trust.

Trust in an organization is the foundation for success. When people trust you they will knock down walls for you. When they don't trust you they will let you down at every opportunity that presents itself. The most effective method to establishing trust is to be trustworthy. It means that you can be counted on when needed. It means that you will maintain confidentiality when appropriate. When you have trust, you cannot help but to be successful and without trust, you are destined to fail.

Authentic leadership means establishing trust with everyone in your organization. If you are trustworthy there is no need for an exercise. If you need to establish trust, start with being honest and develop true, genuine relationships with your team.

Authentic Leadership is trusted leadership.

Say Thank You Often, Both Verbally and in Written Communications

Two words that mean so much and are used so infrequently...thank you

WHEN WAS THE LAST TIME YOU TOLD someone thank you? I say thank you all of the time. It is really a part of my daily conversations. Each time I express gratitude, and sincerity, people are very receptive to it. In fact, they end up smiling when they hear those words.

We all would like to feel valued and appreciated for our efforts. The clerk at the drug store works just as hard as your physician. The service from the waitress in the restaurant is equally important as your attorney's service. When we take the time to give a welcomed response for a task performed well, it initiates a connection. You begin to establish a rapport with the other person. Thank you is a great way to bridge the gap. It is a very effective tool.

Exercise:
Begin to say thank you to everyone that performs a task or service for you. This will include your children, spouse/significant other, your team members, peers etc. You feel great when you say it and they enjoy hearing it.

Saying thank you goes a long way.

If You Say It, You Better Do It

You are a walking billboard for your actions

DID YOU KNOW THAT PEOPLE LISTEN TO what you do? When you tell someone that they must show up on time, you better never be late and, if you are late, you better have a very good reason. If you say that you want a neat and clean area, your office must never be in disarray. When you want excellence from your team then, by all means, you have to deliver excellent leadership.

How much is your word worth? When you say that you are going to complete a task or project, are people confident that it will happen or do they doubt what you are saying?

When you tell someone that you can be counted on to complete a task, project, event etc, you have to follow through with it. I know that we don't like saying, "no", or "I can't". However, it is far better to tell the truth than to commit and then falter on your promise. If you establish a reputation of not standing firm on your word then you lose creditability and authenticity, and you risk becoming untrustworthy.

Exercise:
Practice both keeping your commitments and not taking on more than you can handle. If you want to

and need to say "no", then say it. Because once you commit, you have to see it through. Also practice keeping the standard that you set for your team. Commit to everything that you expect from them. Your words and actions are their example.

All you have are your word and your corresponding actions. When you don't keep your word, everyone loses.

Be Fair and Consistent

Be honest and forthright all of the time
– it really eliminates drama

LIFE MAY NOT BE FAIR, BUT AS A leader you need to be. Everyone on your team deserves the opportunity to excel. I have seen it time and time again. The person that is liked most, receives all of the attention and growth opportunities. The other team members are neglected. It is wrong and if you are doing this or have done it, STOP immediately.

You can't have favorites in your leadership position. It creates conflict. We know that conflict is a cancer that can kill an organization. If you fail to comply, it will surely come back to bite you when you least expect it.

Everyone deserves the opportunity to be great. As a PINK leader it is your responsibility to bring out the best in all of your team members. Treat them all fairly, consistently. Authentic leadership is fair leadership.

Be Objective

Life becomes less complicated when we make decisions based on facts, not emotions.

BEING OBJECTIVE PROVIDES THE LIBERTY to make decisions that are fair and practical. As a leader, when you focus on the facts, it enables you to take out the emotion in the decision making process. The most successful leaders in the world are able to act and make decisions even when they don't feel like it. They are able to do this because facts require objectivity and feelings are based on subjectivity. Beyond a reasonable doubt when you focus on solid, concrete information you make the best decision for yourself, your team, and your organization. The next time you need to make a decision focus on the factual, tangible information and you will make the best decision.

Exercise: Follow these four steps to maintain objectivity when making decisions.

1. *Review all of the information*
2. *Weigh the pro's and con's*
3. *Eliminate emotion*
4. *Make the decision*

The facts are the facts and you can't argue with them. I know you are saying, but one of the realistic focus areas is "your heart". How can you be objective if you need to consider feelings? Here is an example using the three areas, while maintaining objectivity.

1. If you need to promote someone, you use "your head" to review their performance and their qualifications. You promote the most qualified candidate.

2. If someone comes into your office and says they just lost a loved one, then you would use "your heart" to empathize with their loss.

3. If an employee is lying to you, then you would use "your gut" to resolve the issue.

Being objective takes the emotions out. It helps you make the best decision.

Help Others

We all need somebody to lean on

GIVING BACK IS SOWING SEED for your own future. Don't think of helping only as charitable events. If you have the ability to help someone, then you should help them. Helping others goes beyond charity. Help comes in many different forms. A team member may need some assistance with their performance; a friend may need help with their resume or becoming organized; a peer may need some coaching.

Whenever you are asked to help someone, you should see it as an opportunity to further their development. Success is not always about your own path, but about the differences that you make along the way to change the lives of others.

Lend a helping hand whenever and wherever you can.

Exercise Tact

Tact is like a dessert fork, present but used sparingly

EARLY IN MY LEADERSHIP CAREER I was a terrible leader. My only concerns were my own needs. My leadership style consisted of being an arrogant power hungry dictator that was selfish and epitomized tactlessness.

One day during my junior year of high school, we were in JROTC class conducting drill and ceremony activities. There was one cadet that just could not execute the movements correctly. She was getting on my nerves because we could not move on without her. I called her up to the front of the formation and began to yell at her. Everyone started to laugh at her as she had to execute the movements step-by-step, over and over until finally she was so embarrassed, she almost cried. My thought process was that by making her feel low enough she would stop making mistakes. It worked. She finally executed the move correctly and we completed the rest of the training.

The next day my JROTC Sergeant asked me to come into his office and he asked me what the word "tact" meant. My response was that I did not know. He told me to go home and look it up in the dictionary and come back and tell him. I left class, went home, and looked up the word in the dictionary.

The next day I walked into his office and reported back the meaning verbatim. He responded "You were supposed to tell me what you thought the word meant, not repeat the definition to me." Standing in front of him perplexed he told me, "go home and think about it again and tomorrow you better have a more acceptable answer."

The following day, I walked into his office and told him what he wanted to hear by stating, "Leader's need to use tact when yelling at soldiers." He looked at me in disbelief. He was so frustrated with me he almost demoted me.

Once he calmed down, he stated, "YOU do not use tact when working with the cadets." He told me that as a leader this was a necessary skill that needed to be used consistently. Not really understanding what he meant I told him that my goal would be to work on it.

In the early years my inability to use tact was stifled because of my tunnel vision. REAL leaders know that tact requires understanding a perspective outside of your own and then handling it according. Tactful leadership is empathetic and selfless.

As you go up the ladder of success there are all sorts of people along the way and they have a vast array of feelings and points of view. Honing your tact skills will eliminate obstacles that can occur. Let my mistakes be yours so that you don't have to make them. Please use tact as often as you need to.

Admit When You Are Wrong

❦

Apologizing does not weaken your ability to lead

I HATED TO ADMIT BEING WRONG about anything. My preference would be to eat live insects than to admit the error of my ways. To say those three little words caused me to feel like a punk, or an ineffective leader. My belief was that people who said "I am sorry" were actually "sorry." It took years for me to understand the strength that it takes a leader to admit they were wrong and then follow up with an apology.

Most of us don't like to apologize because we first have to admit that we were wrong or have offended someone and that makes us feel uncomfortable. Then to apologize means that we have to look someone in the eye and affirm our error. We don't like it at all. But, think about how the other person feels when you do apologize. They have closure to the situation.

If you have difficulty apologizing you have to let it go. You will become a better leader when you are able to admit errors, correct them, and then move forward. Here is an exercise to assist you with apologizing.

Exercise:
Start practicing apologizing to yourself in the mirror. Say "I apologize/I am sorry" out loud while

looking directly into your eyes. This will enable you to see what others will see when you apologize to them in the future. Continue to practice this exercise until you feel comfortable and then you can begin to apologize as the need arises.

There is great strength in admitting when you are wrong. This is a secret that all PINK leaders know and understand.

Leader Led

The best way to lead is from the front, while bringing your team along with you. This is accomplished by being the example that you want others to follow. If you want excellence, you need to exude excellence. If you want your team to follow, you must show them where they are going; you will need to be with them every step of the way.

Your actions in being leader led will no doubt speak louder than your words.

Lead by Example

※

Be the example that you want others to follow

GREAT LEADERS ARE THE EXAMPLE. In all of their essence and glory, they are effective listeners and very approachable, appearing real and genuine. Their skills are unparalleled and they provide sound advice that is value added. They mystify us with how they are able to find a way to tap into the potential of every person on the team, in a manner that makes them feel valued and appreciated. They are in an elite group.

Think about the leaders you have had in your life. We all have had a leader that we would have climbed to the top of Mount Everest with. The leaders that we feel compelled to follow lead by example. When we see our leaders doing what they ask, we know that, first and foremost, it can be accomplished. We also know that they have what it takes to lead us.

In essence, to bring out the best in your team they need to witness the best in you. When you demonstrate the skills to achieve success, your team will be right there with you ready, willing, and able to follow you to victory.

As a warehouse supervisor, the goal was to learn how to perform every job task enabling me to understand what the work felt like for my team members. Knowing the daily challenges that they faced helped me to lead them effectively. On days when we had multiple call offs I would fill in to help complete the work on time and the team appreciated my work efforts. Being leader led means that you have to be willing to do what you are asking your team to do.

Exercise:
List the areas that you are currently leading by example.

_____

_____

_____

_____

_____

_____

_____

_____

List one area that you need to focus on to lead by example.

_____

_____

_____

_____

_____

_____

_____

_____

Develop action plans to begin to focus on the area that need work.

_____

_____

_____

_____

_____

_____

_____

Once you have completed the action plans, begin to lead your team to accomplish organizational goals.

If you want excellence from your team then you need to demonstrate excellent leadership. Become the leader that you want to follow up Mount Everest.

Inspect What You Expect

Excellence will occur in the areas where you focus

DURING MY MILITARY CAREER THERE was a valuable lesson learned. The soldiers only cleaned what they knew would be inspected nothing more and nothing less. Whenever we returned from the field or training, there was an inspection of vehicles, equipment and weapons it was a routine inspection.

One day before the weapons inspection the platoon sergeant told me to inspect every soldier's butt stock (the bottom on the weapon). Prior to this day none of the soldiers were ever asked to open the bottom of their weapons. The assumption was that they were using this area for its intended purpose, which was to store their weapons cleanings kit in it.

I walked up to the first soldier and started inspecting his weapon in my routine sequence. Just as he was about to take his weapon back, I asked the soldier to open the butt stock of the weapon. He looked at me as if he had seen a ghost. He asked me to repeat the request then he opened it up. At that moment trash fell onto the ground and there was more dirt in the storage area. Between the trash and the dirt, there was no room for a weapons cleaning kit. The inspection continued revealing more of the same dirt and trash in the butt stocks.

Once the inspection was finished the platoon could sense the disappointment. I promised to eliminate the routine. We would follow military guidelines but never in the same sequence twice. Of course you are thinking that it was my soldier's fault that they were not cleaning their weapons entirely. It was not their fault.

PINK leaders understand that soldiers, team members and even other leaders are only going to do what is expected. The expectation was never set in the platoon that they needed to clean their butt stocks and store their cleaning kit in the butt stock. This was a task that they learned in Basic Training but, after that training no one ever inspected the butt stock again. It simply became an expectation. The end state was a dirty butt stock filled with trash.

That event inspired me to begin to inspect everything office space, lockers, warehouses, equipment, vehicles, and dumpsters. If I am responsible for it, I inspect it frequently. When something is not meeting the standard on the spot coaching is given immediately. It is a lot of work for me but everyone that I lead knows what is expected. This standard of excellence has resulted in winning numerous competitions, and awards.

PINK leadership is the belief that mediocrity is the enemy to high standards.

Exercise:
Think about a process or system in your organization that needs to addressed, now develop action plans that will enable you and the team to take the area to

a higher level. Be sure to include details of timing and who will perform what task.

_____

_____

_____

_____

_____

_____

_____

_____

_____

_____

_____

_____

_____

_____

_____

_____

_____

As you begin to gain momentum in one area start to focus on other areas until your entire team or organization is performing at a high level.

Visualize Your Goals

When you see it, you can believe it, so write it down

1. Become a great leader.
2. Learn to play the piano.
3. Earn my doctorate.
4. Start my own business.
5. Get married and have children.

THESE WERE JUST A FEW OF THE goals on my success list. The origin of the list came about during my time in the military. The list is commonly referred to as "the list of 25." The goals on the list are professional and personal. Referring to the list often helps me to stay focused on my goals. There are several copies of the list to be placed in key areas, the wallet, the house, the office. When goals have been accomplished they are crossed off the list and replaced with new ones.

There is just something about seeing goal's written down that makes it a reality. It is almost contractual you are telling yourself that you have to accomplish this task. When you write it down you are making a commitment. Whatever your success path is, start writing down your goals that will enable you to live out your dreams. You will begin to focus on them when you can refer to them continually. Where your focus lies is where you are bound to travel.

Exercise:
Write down what you want to achieve as a leader professionally and personally. Capture everything from becoming an effective listener to winning a prestigious award; whatever it is that you equate to success. A list of 8-10 goals are realistic until you are comfortable using the list. Once the list is completed, make copies of it and post it everywhere. Refer to it throughout your day. The constant daily reminder will enable you to focus on it and then you will achieve it. As you complete the goal cross them off the list and develop new goals. Continue this process throughout your career. You will accomplish more and achieve greater success because you are tracking your goals.

Did you know that you are 80-90% more likely to accomplish your goals when you write them down? You have to be able to visualize your success it is all about seeing it.

Begin to visualize your leadership success and make it a reality by writing it down.

Learn to Say "We"

❋

"I" will only get you so far, "we" will take you to the end

I WOULD WALK INTO MEETINGS WITH my platoon when I was in the Army and I would tell them what "I" was going to do. You know what...they let met. They let me do all that "I" could do. After a couple of months of doing it by myself, "I" was exhausted. I realized that that "I" needed help so I quickly learned to say "we." Now whenever I am talking about anything that requires help from someone else, I start with "We".

Teams trust leaders that say "we." It simply feels like a group effort. Using "we" brings a since of cohesiveness that ensures maximum participation. When you speak in "we" terms you immediately are able to gain participation from the group. Those that are apart of the "we" feel a sense of belonging. They know that they are not alone in the task and are focused on goal attainment. If you are a leader like "I" use to be. Stop focusing on "I" and starting looking at "we," I guarantee that your results will improve immensely.

Exercise:
Eliminate the usage of the word "I" whenever talking to your team. Take a jar and label it, "The I Jar," then place it on your desk in plain view. Every time

you find yourself saying "I" put a dollar in it. Let everyone know that you and your fellow leaders are eliminating the use of the word "I" whenever it refers to the team or the organization. Once the "I's" have been eliminated, take the money from the jar and throw the "Team" a party.

Tell your team together "we" can achieve success.

Be Willing to Follow Someone Else

❧

Those that lead successfully were followers first

AT 15 YEARS OLD I MADE THE decision to become a leader. In JROTC leadership for me meant, calling the shots, bossing everyone around and becoming a Colonel. Ironically being a PINK leader has nothing to with shot calling and bossing folks around. The foundation of effective leadership is the result of good "followership."

My JROTC instructor sat down with me one day because my squad was having difficulties with my leadership style. They were unwilling to be led. He informed me that as a squad member I did not follow my leader which is why my squad was not following me. He also stated that in order to lead you must first learn how to follow. Those were his last words before he demoted me and then took my squad. To make matters worse, he made me a member of the same squad again. The demotion was devastating.

My squad did not make it easy either; there was constant ridicule about me becoming a squad member again. They teased and laughed at me every day during class. As a result, I hated JROTC after the demotion.

After a couple of weeks, three epiphanies later, and on the verge of quitting, my mother told me that she had not raised a quitter. Inspired by her words I decided to listen to my JROTC instructor and became a follower with the sole purpose of understanding what it meant to be a team player. The remainder of the semester was spent learning how to follow.

The next school year when promoted to squad leader, the squad followed me. From that point on my leadership skills began to develop and by my senior year the goal of being a Colonel was achieved; making me the third highest ranking officer in JROTC. The great performance demonstrated in JROTC led to a ROTC scholarship followed by a Commission to the U.S. Army in the Military Police Corps.

When my JROTC instructor removed me from my squad leader position, quitting the program was the first thought that came to mind. He "fired" me! Looking back on the situation it makes perfect sense why the demotion was necessary. It was a very effective leadership experience. A PINK leader requires more than the ability to tell others what to do. They must be able to take orders first before giving them.

The best leaders were the best followers first.

Be the Best

❦

You're going for it, you might as well be the best

THE PHILOSOPHY THAT I HAVE followed since I was 21 years old is "Be the best and do not settle for less." My goal is to work very diligently to ensure that I am giving 110%. It is my belief that when you are focused on being the best you are constantly in growth mode. It requires that you are always innovative, being on the leading edge and moving forward. As you strive to be the best you inspire those around you to become their best. It creates a positive winning atmosphere that breeds sustainable success for excellence that everyone feels compelled to follow.

Athletes are a great example of understanding this principle. Kobe Bryant is the best because he lives, eats and breaths basketball. There are also other great people that have worked to be the best in sports and other industries. Tiger Woods, Michael Jordan, Donald Trump, Oprah, Warren Buffet, Bill Gates, Deepak Chopra, John Wooden, Tony Robbins, Nelson Mandela, Suzie Orman, and the list goes on. They enjoy what they do and they are very good at it. They are the best in their fields because they consistently strive for excellence.

Exercise: How to become the best.

Being the best means everything that you touch is your best effort. It is as simple as an email to as great as rolling out a change plan. You have to commit that everything you touch will turn to gold. Your reputation must be that wherever you go excellence will follow. You have to commit that everything you do in all areas of your life will be "your best." Put your best effort forward starting now. Presenting your best consistently will enable you to become you best.

Start today with one area that you can improve upon; when it becomes your best, move on to the next area. Keep the momentum going until your natural habit is to strive for excellence continually.

Delegate

The art of reducing stress is to delegate

MY PERCEPTION OF DELEGATION WAS that it meant you were lazy or incompetent. As a young officer the mere thought of delegating was freighting. How would anyone see my competence if everyone else was doing my job? The full credit for the work needed to go to the leader. Looking back it was a ridiculous mindset but, chalk it up to being 22 years old.

While in the military, completing every task alone caused me sheer exhaustion and everyone else in the platoon was rested and bored. The need to be in control was killing me. Finally, my platoon sergeant told me to begin to trust the leaders within my platoon and they would be effective when given tasks. With some apprehension I let go and began to assign tasks to my squad leaders this ensued great confidence in them, initiating a full blown delegation spree. It was a great decision they were empowered eliminating my exhaustion.

The greatest lesson learned during that time was that, by not delegating nothing was getting accomplished. When I began to delegate everything was taken care of. Delegation also empowered my leaders and developed my coaching and mentoring skills. It was a win for all of us.

Relinquish control and begin to delegate, it really is an effective method.

Remove Obstacles

Success is on the other side of an obstacle,
go over it, go around it, or move it

WHEN WE ARE DRIVING AND WE SEE an obstruction in the middle of the road, our gut tells us that we need to go around the obstacle. Within seconds we are looking for an out, to either go around it or move to another lane. If either of those options will not work, as a last resort we position our wheels to drive over it. Our natural instincts are amazing we miss the obstruction and we continue to drive without giving it a second thought.

Our own lives are no different. When obstacles occur as they will in life we view them differently than road obstructions. We want to know why this is happening to us, why does it have to be so difficult to achieve success. We begin to compare ourselves to others and how much easier they have it. News flash everyone in life has their own set of obstacles to overcome. They may address them privately or differently however, everyone has obstacles to overcome and that's a fact!

My method to obstacle removal is simple. See them all as obstructions in the road that you must safely maneuver past to travel to your destination. Follow your gut; it will always guide you around, over or through the obstacles.

PINK leaders effectively navigate through obstacles, to reach success on the other side.

Think Positive

❈

The power of positive thinking always prevails

YOU HAVE TWO OPTIONS EACH day when you wake up, you can think negatively or positively. Which ever option you choose your day will follow your thoughts. Deciding to think positive gives you optimism. When you have an optimistic mindset you are able to capitalize from every situation. The old adage is very true, "When life gives you lemons, make lemonade…then sell it for a profit."

I am constantly looking for new methods to put a positive spin on in every area of my life. My divorce was life altering and yet there was still a need for me to celebrate. My goal was to celebrate key events that were a result of the divorce. I celebrate the anniversary of my divorce every year, because of my growth and my emotional progress. The career success for me has been achieved because of the skills that were developed during and after the divorce. There have also been growth opportunities because of difficult experiences in Corporate America.

My career in Corporate America was almost lost twice because there was conflict between myself and my supervisors. Each day, there was growth by telling myself that this was simply a way to learn how to handle conflict head on. Because of my positive mindset I survived and after working for each of the supervisors my next positions were promotions.

Over the years I have just come to know that things are going to happen. If you live in the world difficult moments are inevitable. You have the option to embrace it and work through it, or you can sit in it and sulk. Life is so much better when you find the good in every situation. If you spend too much time thinking negative thoughts you make obstacles that will hinder your ability to excel. Living a successful life means that you possess the ability to get past any situation and prevail as long as you maintain a positive attitude.

PINK leaders think positive constantly.

Provide Coaching

✠

The teams that win consistently have the best coaches

GROWING UP WE WERE NOT TAUGHT the skill of being an effective coach. My mother instructed us to perform a task and we complied. When she gave an order, there was no dialogue about what support was needed or how to effectively carry out the order. If we failed to complete the task we did not talk about what thought process we used, or how we could have done things differently. We knew for certain that there were consequences and repercussions for non compliance.

Don't misconstrue me, my mother was great; she is a significant part of my success. However, she is "old school" and there is not a coaching bone in her body. Believe me coaching is a learned skill, if it were left up to my mother to teach me how to coach effectively, this book would have been two pages. Page one, "do it", page two, "or else..." Fortunately for me effective coaching was taught in the military and in Corporate America.

What is great about being a coach is that you have to transfer your knowledge and skills to someone else. Coaching requires that you convince others that they have the necessary skills to perform a task to the best of their capabilities; letting them know that they can win when they work hard. John Wooden in my opinion is the greatest example of effective coaching. I can only aspire to coach at that level.

PINK leaders love coaching. They enjoy working through the challenges that present themselves along the way. The transformation that takes place when a team performs at their next level is very rewarding. Coaching is one of the greatest leadership positions that you will ever have.

When you coach you learn as much as those that you are leading.

Preparation is the Key

⋅ ❈ ⋅

Dare to prepare, it will take you everywhere

WE HAVE ALL BEEN GUILTY OF IT. Waiting until the last minute and then throwing something together; whether it is a meal, an outfit, a speech, a presentation, a document or a project. When we have finished, we know that we did not put forth our best effort and sometimes it works and most often it does not. If we have been successful in "pulling it off," we feel as though we got away with it. In essence we have cheated ourselves and those that were part of the event.

When you take the time to prepare, you present the best. You look your best, the meals taste great, the presentation or speech was effective and the participants walked away enlightened. Success is not about how you can fake your way through. It is all about sustainability and never about irresponsibility. If you truly want to be a successful leader then it will take time and it will also require that you prepare for everything consistently.

My entire schedule changed because of starting my own company. The most significant change was to change my sleeping schedule to going to bed early and waking up very early. Sufficient rest is necessary for me to have a fresh state of mind to make the best decisions for my clients. The only way for me to be effective in providing great service is to be prepared. These changes to my schedule ensure that I am at my best.

Your success is totally dependent upon how much you are willing to prepare yourself and everything that represents who you are. When you truly become committed to being successful then you take the time that is needed to prepare. You will present your best all of the time and your commitment to preparation will benefit yourself as well as those that you lead.

Prepare, Prepare, Prepare.... Did I mention prepare? Preparation is being proactive, it is taking the time to do it right.

Procrastination is being reactive it is putting tasks off until they have to be completed.

Leverage Your Experts

There are people that know the answer, stop straining your brain and ask the experts

HAVE YOU EVER TRIED TO FIX YOUR computer on your own? How many hours did you work on it before you realized you needed the help of an expert? Don't answer out loud, would not want to make you feel bad. We all have tried to work on something, a car, an appliance, a computer etc. knowing that we are not good at it. The question is why? Maybe we don't want to feel like we need the help of someone else. It makes us feel powerless if we have to ask for assistance.

From this moment forward, when you want to know something, ask those that already have the answer. Success is about knowing your own skill level and when your need goes beyond that level, seek the help of an expert. It will save you time and energy and make your life easier.

Ask the experts because they do have the answer. Stop trying to be a Jack of all trades and a Master of none. Specialize and let the experts take care of the rest.
PINK leaders know their strengths and capabilities anything out of their scope they seek the expertise, advice and knowledge of others.

Hold Yourself and Others Accountable

Accountability: without it we are reckless

ACCOUNTABILITY IS TWO-FOLD. When the team is doing well then you provide great rewards and recognition. Conversely, when the team is not performing then as their leader you need to provide coaching, training and discipline.

View accountability in this manner:

1. Reward and recognize when things are going well.
2. Coach, train, mentor discipline when performance is off track.

It is much easier to let things slide. There is a tremendous amount of effort needed to keep everyone focused and on track. PINK leaders enjoy holding people accountable because without it, we all have the potential to become reckless.

In the military soldiers could have died without being held accountable for their actions. In business there can be significant losses of profit and lives if we neglect our duties. Enron is the perfect example of lack of accountability. Thousands of people lost their life savings and retirement because no one stood up and said "This is wrong we need to stop."

REAL leaders set high accountability standards, for everyone in the organization. Accountability ranks high in their book. Leveraging it, greatness can be achieved, without it organizations are destined to fail. Holding others accountable may be a challenge for you but, in your strive for excellence know that accountability must become an integral part of your inner fiber.

Being leader led means consistently holding yourself and others accountable.

Reprimand Privately

❈

The end result of open reprimand is resentment

"YELLER, POWER HUNGRY, difficult" were the characteristics used to describe my leadership style during the early JROTC years. The tactic of embarrassing other cadets was my idea of effective leadership. The result was that the cadets began to resent me because of the constant scrutiny that they were placed under. After being on the receiving end of embarrassment and reprimanding put a whole new perspective on my leadership style.

During a meeting while stationed in Korea my Company Commander embarrassed my entire platoon. He basically told us that we were the worst platoon in the company and we were dragging the Company's reputation down. The other three platoons stood there and laughed at us. We just stood there and took my Commander's comments. After the incident, I was very angry and wanted revenge.

Days after my Commander's antic's my platoon continued to experience constant ridicule. I decided to bring my platoon in and told them that we were the best and we were going to prove it. They needed to understand that the Commander's statements were not true and that the best way to prove someone wrong was to show them.

We set out to be the best in every area. We were the 1st platoon out of four; our motto became "First platoon second to none." By the end of the year my platoon was the best in the company.

Once back on U.S. soil I swore to never intentionally reprimand someone publically ever again. My commander's words hurt but, the laughing from everyone else hurt even more. PINK leaders never intentionally hurt or embarrass. When you need to discipline or reprimand a team member or leader, take the time to do it behind closed doors.

Leverage Your Strengths and Understand Your Weaknesses

❋

When you are strong you will excel

I KNOW AND UNDERSTAND WHAT my strengths and weaknesses are. Great focus should be placed on your areas of strength. You will need to work on your weaknesses to maintain balance but, leverage your strengths to achieve success.

Here is an example:

I am not good at assembling things somehow when the project is completed there are always extra pieces left over. As a result, my mantra is, "No assembly is a requirement." If I have to put it together it is not purchased. When buying my daughter her first bike, we went to the store and looked at the display bike. We both liked it and it was in our price range. We asked the sales person for the bike and he walked us down the isle where the bikes were located in a box. I told him that the bike needed to come assembled. He informed me that we would have to put the bike together. My response was "I am willing to pay extra to have it assembled," he told me that service was not available. We left the store.

We then proceeded to go to the next store. There was a bike very similar to her first selection. I asked the clerk about the bike he told me that it was the last one, and it was on sale which was an added bonus. My daughter liked it and it was already assembled. The bike was paid for and my daughter rode it out of the store. We both left satisfied.

You see I could have purchased the first bike and tired to put it together and it would have never worked. We both would have become frustrated, my daughter would not have had a bike for the summer and neither of us would have been very happy. I am terrible with assembling parts it is not enjoyable and makes me upset hence the mantra, "no assembly required."

There are groups that believe that you should work on your weaknesses to become stronger but it really is not effective. We all are equipped to do certain things well and there are other things that we will never be good at and that is okay. That is why we have experts in every industry. When you have to operate in an area of weakness, ask for support and do your best to make it through. Your ultimate goal should be to spend the bulk of your time focused on areas you are strong in. Your success will come from your strengths so leverage them as often as possible.

My voice is my strength and I work within the confines of it. Assembly is my greatest weakness. I use my voice to ask others to assemble.

Talk to People, Not at Them

· ✤ ·

There is a big difference between a demand and a request

JROTC afforded me the opportunity to tell people what to do. It felt good ordering the cadets around. Walking around all day long giving commands/demands felt good. It was instant gratification for me when someone cringed at the sound of my voice. Ruling by fear really led me to believe that the cadets were being developed. The more they were belittled and demeaned the better it made me feel. Needless to say the lesson for me was to learn how to talk to the cadets.

My initial communication method was very disrespectful, even though my rank was higher than other cadet's they were still human beings and deserved to be treated with respect. Through effective coaching and developing I learned that it is far better to request than to demand.

Today I understand that there is a distinct difference in talking at a person and talking to them. Talking at them puts up barriers and causes internal conflict and resentment. Talking to people creates open dialogue and builds relationships. Talking at them implies that they do not have feelings and they don't matter. Talking at someone is harsh and crude. Talking to them requires empathy and the ability to listen. It clearly is the most effective method to communicate.

Examples:

Talking at someone:

Go get the presentation

Talking to someone:

Can you please look on my desk and bring a copy of the presentation? I need it for the conference call today.

PINK Leaders talk to people enabling them to achieve positive results.

Powerful

A powerful leader needs to innovate, motivate, mentor, inspire change, develop and challenge those that they lead. This is easy when things are going well. However, when the going gets tough a powerful leader is able to dig deep and persevere and lead themselves and their organization to victory.

As a powerful leader, you must never give up or quit. Your success is derived from your ability to draw from your power to achieve excellence. Your power begins with three letters, c-a-n.

Can Makes the Impossible, Possible

If the little engine could do it, then so can you

HAVE YOU EVER HEARD anyone make the following statements?

a. That's impossible.
b. No one has ever been able to accomplish that.
c. He is too short to play basketball.
d. No man has ever been able to do it.
e. No woman has ever been able to do it.

Here are responses to those statements:

a. Run a mile in less than four minutes.
b. Win 8 Olympic Medals.
c. Spud Webb.
d. Walk on the moon.
e. Fly around the world.

Never let anyone tell you that something can't be done. It only takes a change in your thought process from: "I can't", to "How can I?" When you tell yourself that you can do it, you will.

Thinking PINK makes all things possible.

Swim Upstream

You develop new strengths when you are faced with adversity

WHEN YOU THINK OF THE PHRASE, "swimming upstream," the first thought that comes to mind is that, it is a difficult task that no one really wants to perform.

I have often thought about what it would mean to arrive on land after swimming upstream......

I would be stronger after swimming through the rough water having greater use of my five senses; they were heightening in my need to survive the swim. My mind would be sound because of the focus that it took to make it to my destination. My confidence would have increased because the challenge was completed.

Swimming upstream.... Maybe it's worth a try.

The next time you are faced with a difficulty or a challenge don't resist, embrace it by thinking of how you will have benefited by sticking it out.

Swimming upstream is great exercise!

Quitters Never Win

When you quit, the person that loses the most is you

AS A SOPHOMORE IN HIGH school I quit the track team because I was not good at running. Of course my story was that my grades were slipping because of track. Everyone knew that the story was a lie. The truth was that I sucked and it was very apparent.

During the summer of my junior and senior year of high school I went to the Army and attended Basic Training for six weeks. Upon returning home I had grown mentally, physically and emotionally as a result of the experience. The new found strength caused me to want to go back to school and run track again. I did not want to graduate from high school having quit the track team.

The first day of school registration the meeting with the track coach went well and she could sense that this time around things were going to be different for me. The first day of practice everyone was shocked by my presence. I was not back for their approval so their stares went unacknowledged. Coming back was to prove that succeeding was a possibility.

The season approach taken was totally different, I worked hard during practices and pushed myself to new limits by lifting weights and changing eating habits. More focus was placed on lettering and winning races which was something I was not successful at during my sophomore year.

At the end of the track season the following goals were achieved, lettering in cross country and the regular season, 3 bronze medals and one silver medal, one second improvement in the 200m and 2 feet improvement in the long jump. By staying focused and not quitting a new standard of excellence was accomplished. The proof was in the results I was not a quitter and the season was a great success.

A couple of years ago I was visiting a city track meet and the coach for the men's team was still coaching at my old high school. He told me that even though I was not the best runner on the team I had heart and never gave up. His statement made me feel good because he remembered the tenacity demonstrated.

Looking back at the photo's of me competing sparks a since of pride. I could have graduated from high school and went to college and never ran in a track meet again. It really would not have made a difference. But, by going back I gained the experience that organized sports encompassed. The friendships made were invaluable as well.

I am not suggesting that you go back and right the wrongs of your youth however you need to see things through until completion. The lesson is in the experience. Trust me you will excel more in the areas that you are strong in. But, you will learn more when you are presented with a challenge that is so difficult it makes you want to quit. When you push through the anxiety that comes from feeling like you will fail success is waiting for you, on the other side.

PINK leaders push themselves to a higher performance. They are winners because they do not quit.

Exercise:
Every time that you are faced with a challenge or an obstacle, repeat the statement listed below:

I _____ am not a quitter. I will work towards my goal and I will win. No matter what I encounter along the way I will preserver. I am not a quitter. I am a winner!

Persevere During Times of Adversity

Your greatest strengths arise when you are most vulnerable

LET'S FACE IT, WE HATE adversity. No one walks around saying come on difficult moments I am ready for you. We don't wake up in the morning telling ourselves, "I want at least three overwhelming events to occur before 9 o'clock this morning." This is not our reality however, what is real is that, difficult moments will occur.

We are confronted with challenges and adverse times in all areas of our lives. Each one of us has stories that we could share. Do you realize that the stories are just as important as the outcome? Talking about my divorce was one of the most vicissitude moments in my life, but it helps to show the wins that can occur when you preserve.

During those months of the divorce, I was mentally, physically and emotionally at my weakest. Waking up in the morning was difficult. However, each day that I persevered made me become stronger. Somehow I managed and over time it became easier. The weight of the divorce became lighter. Walking through the pain was the most effective method to make it through to the other side.

To be honest, there were days throughout my healing that I just wanted to give in and go hide in a closet to cry myself to sleep. But, something deep on the inside of me would not allow me to quit; besides quitting never solved anything. For me there was more to life than losing a husband.

Success comes during those times when outside influences cannot move you from your path. When you find that you are faced with work or personal issues you have to dig deep within and find that voice that tells you, "don't give up," and "that which does not kill you makes you stronger." By working through the situation you will be better equipped to handle future issues that will come about.

You have everything you need to be persistent in moments of duress. The secret is in knowing that you can do it. You simply have to tell yourself that it is possible even when the outlook seems bleak. It is in those thoughts that you will tap into your power.

Failure is Not an Option

· ✖ ·

*Falling down is the easy part, the challenge is
to succeed once you have gotten up*

GUESS WHAT, IF YOU FALL DOWN you don't have to stay down. Get up, dust yourself off and keep going. I have never admitted the following failures to strangers prior to writing this book. My belief is that it is necessary as the reader for you to understand how my failures never stopped me from achieving my goals. Here is a list of a few failures:

1. Failed the run portion of my first physical fitness test when I was in Basic Training.
2. Failed the written portion of my driver's license test twice.
3. Fired from a temp position after graduating from college because I could not answer a nine line phone system.
4. Failed the GRE the first two times that I took it.
5. Failed the third phase of Air Assault School as a Captain in the U.S. Army.

I got up from every failure and here are the results:

1. Achieved a perfect score during the run on my final physical fitness test before I left the Army.
2. Passed all driving test since then.
3. Never been fired from a job again and can answer multiple phone lines if necessary.
4. Have a Doctorate in Organizational Leadership after taking the GRE three times.
5. Earned my Air Assault badge after completing the third phase for the second time.

I have failed and succeeded. Never once letting the failures stop me from moving forward. Sure the failures hurt. They were embarrassing and made me feel like crap each time it occurred. But, what felt much better was getting up and succeeding. Accepting the failures as a challenge allowed me to overcome them.

That is how you need to view failure. You have to tell your self that failure is not an option.

A PINK leader has only one option and that is to succeed.

Innovative

Successful leadership is about taking the team and the organization to the next level this is possible with innovation. I like to refer to innovation as invigoration. As a leader when you develop a new concept or idea you change the performance culture; new ideas bring new life to you, your team and your organization. Great things occur when a team brainstorms the next big thing.

Innovation brings fun and excitement to the organization.

Have Fun

Success is better when you are having fun

HERE'S THE BIGGEST SECRET ABOUT success...you can have fun while you are working towards accomplishing your goals. The misconception is that if you are really focused on becoming successful there is no time to enjoy it. However, this is the perfect time to enjoy the ride on the success train. If you dread what you are doing on your way to achieving success, then you will not enjoy the success when it is achieved. I challenge you to find the excitement and joy in every event.

Exercise:
1. Write down 3 ways that you can enjoy becoming a successful leader

_____

_____

_____

_____

_____

_____

---

2. Write down 3 things that your team / employees can do to make their jobs fun

---

Share the list with one another and hold each other accountable to having fun continuously.

Embrace Diversity

Diversity is what makes us unique, and it makes life interesting

WHAT IS THE FIRST THOUGHT THAT comes to your mind when you hear the word diversity? Quite often when you hear the term diversity you will naturally think of race or ethnicity. But it is so much more than that. There are characteristics that are visible and traits that are not visible that we include in diversity.

Here is a list of some of my diverse characteristics:

Black
Female
From an urban city
Veteran
Parent
Christian
Middle aged
Athletic
Educated
Divorced

You understand the point.

We need to challenge ourselves and leave our comfort zone and truly embrace diversity to be successful. The most fascinating aspect of diversity is that it is limitless. When you encounter someone that is different from you, take the time to learn about your differences. Find out what a magnificent person they are because they are not like you. You will become well rounded and you will expand your network when you take the time to embrace diversity.

Exercise:
Locate 5 new people that are very different from you. I suggest the following diverse characteristics: age, gender, marital status, tenure, geographical location, educational background, experience, socioeconomic status, and technical competence are used as the screening criteria. Once you have identified these five people you are going to establish effective genuine relationships with them. You will become well rounded and broaden your own diversity.

Every PINK Leader has a diversity portfolio.

Stop Working and Start Achieving

Work can be hard when we resist it,
when we focus on achieving it becomes rewarding

JUST THINK ABOUT THE WORD work, it just sounds hard. "I have to go to work, that sure was hard work, and all I do is work." None of those statements make you want to work. The next statements sound better, "Today I excelled by accomplishing my goal. My meeting was very effective today. I finished everything on my to-do-list and three things that were not on it." The latter sentences all required work but they did not sound or feel like work. Furthermore, the events sounded as if they were rewarding accomplishments.

When you change your mindset to believe that you are achieving and that you are not simply working, you can and will accomplish more. Sure everyone has tasks that they loath. You can get through them by looking at what will be gained once the task has been completed. Success is about singles and doubles. There may not always be a homerun in every task. You have to celebrate the wins in every accomplishment. When you look at your career and life as accomplishments then it no longer feels like work.

Reward Openly

Open praise is a great form of flattery

RAISE YOUR HAND IF YOU DON'T like to be rewarded for your success. Not too many people fit into that category. We like to receive praise for a job well done. I will be the first to admit winning and being rewarded for it feels great.

In my opinion, adults do not receive rewards often enough. Think about all of the achievement rewards you received as a child in school. Somehow we have lost the sense of celebration in our organizations. That is why it is very important to reward your team members and their accomplishments. When someone has performed well, attained a goal or gone above and beyond, they should be rewarded. They deserve praise and recognition.

Rewards can be formal and informal. They can come in all forms of praise and recognition, team lunches, dinners, gift cards, certificates, days off, thank you cards, recognition letters sent to their homes, etc. You will be surprised at how recognition can take a person's performance to the next level. Not to mention rewards are a great morale booster. Take the time to recognize your top performers and your team. Your entire organization will benefit.

Exercise:

When you are rewarding someone, present the reward to the honoree in front of their family, friends, peers and leaders. It brings further support to the honoree's performance. I also recommend that you frequently tell your team when they are performing well. In fact look in the mirror every morning and give yourself praise. It is good to hear it no matter what venue you are receiving it from. Rewards make people feel good and it inspires them to want to accomplish more.

REAL leaders recognize great performance as often as they can.

Be Forward Thinking

The greatest chess players win because they are always several moves ahead of their opponents

---

WHERE ARE YOU TAKING YOUR team/organization? Do you know? Where will the company be in 5, 10, 15 years? What challenges will you need to overcome? Where will the market be for your services?

PINK Leader's understand that in order to sustain success they are in constant thinking mode. Your sustainability lies in your ability to think well into the future.

Exercise:
Begin to plan where you are taking yourself, your team and your organization. Put the events on a calendar and stay close to the objectives, ensuring that you are accomplishing them.

Continue to think forward. The future will be here before you know it.

Challenge Yourself

*The only limits that we have are
the ones that we place on ourselves*

WHEN WAS THE LAST TIME THAT you gave yourself a
challenge? Did you complete the challenge? If yes, great.
If no, then why not? Adults often lose sight of the thrill of
a challenge. We often become bored, yet we will not
push ourselves to the next level. I have yet to fully
understand why that is.

I talk with people all of the time and they are in jobs
that they abhor. They want to move and won't. They
want to lose weight but can't seem to find the
motivation. They have always wanted to write a book,
start their own business or travel and they never seem to
have the time. In life when you become stagnant you stop
growing and when you stop growing you begin to
diminish. The answer to stagnation is challenge.

When we are being challenged, our senses are being
used. We have to leverage different resources; we have
to break out of the routine to complete the challenge.
Reality shows are so popular now because they challenge
the contestants. They push them to another level. We
watch in excitement because we want the contestants to
be successful. We feel that they should win because they
are working hard.

Our own lives are no different. Break out of your comfort zone and accept a new challenge. See it all the way to completion.

Exercise:
Accept a challenge in your life; while you are going through the challenge, journal daily to review your progress and growth. When you have completed the challenge journal how you feel.

Set four challenges a year that you have to complete quarterly. In time you will have accomplished a great deal and your ability to achieve success will improve. It is my recommendation that you begin with small challenges and as you build momentum strive for greater tasks.

When you push yourself to the next level, you grow.

Develop a Vision

You will know where you are going when you can visualize it

MY VISION IS, "MEET YOUR Potential." I believe that if everyone focused on meeting their potential, they would achieve greatness. Michael Jordon is one of the greatest basketball players of all time. Oprah Winfrey is a media mogul. Donald Trump has taken the real estate industry to a new level. Warren Buffet is a financial genius. Bill Gates transformed computer software. All of these great minds went after their passion and achieved global success. They created visions for themselves and their organizations and they met their potential and are witnesses to their visions coming to true.

Exercise:
In your drive to success, sit down and develop a vision.

_____

_____

_____

_____

_____

_____

_____

_____

Your vision should be simple, yet focused. It should have meaning to you and those that will follow you. It needs to create a desire, enabling you to move forward. Once you have developed your vision, post it everywhere. Say it many times throughout the day so that it begins to sink down into your subconscious mind. Once it is there continue to live it until it becomes your reality.

Your vision is a roadmap to your success.

Natural

The key to successful leadership is that you have to do what feels natural and good for you. Natural leadership means that you focus on enhancing who you already are. As you work towards achieving leadership success stay true to your values and beliefs; your natural talent will flourish.

Grow Continually

There is a direct correlation between
success and prosperity...growth

TRYING TO ACHIEVE SUCCESS without growth is like climbing a mountain without an air supply. It will never work. We often resist growth in the same capacity as change. We like our lives simple and status quo because growth can be uncomfortable. Growth is a natural progression that when we allow it to come into our lives we can only benefit from its presence.

Think of a child teething. The process is long, arduous, and can take several weeks. The child cries incessantly while the teeth break the skin and reveal themselves. During that time, the child and the parents are miserable. However, once the teeth are in everyone is excited. The parents no longer have to feel helpless as their child suffers through the pain. The child is able to eat solid foods. The new teeth have broadened their palate and they experience a new sensation from food.

The child's parents were not able to explain to them the benefits of teething. The pain of growing the teeth was a necessity to increase their food selection and consumption. The child found out the benefit of having teeth after enduring the pain. Notice that it was after the growth that the child understood the blessing of having teeth.

We don't like how growing feels while it is occurring. However, once the process is completed we enjoy the results. The challenge most leaders face is feeling compelled to grow. We all have an internal clock that triggers an act of growth. We have to become attuned to the clock and when the alarm rings we cannot press the snooze button. When we answer the alarm we should feel excited as we wake up the next evolution of our growth process.

Eliminate / Minimize Stress

※

Stress creates more stress, which creates more stress,
which creates duress

THE STRESS IN OUR LIVES CAN stifle growth and development. You will need to assess every indication of stress in your life and work diligently to minimize or totally eliminate it. When you are stressed, you cannot focus and if you are not focused, then you cannot accomplish your goals.

Exercise:
When I feel stressed identifying the root cause of the stressor(s), helps to resolve it.

> *Step 1: Write down every possible factor that is inducing the stress.*
> *Step 2: Once the list has been compiled, begin to determine if the stress is professional or personal.*
> *Step 3: Rate the stress from 1 – 10. The lowest number equates to less stress, the highest number generates greater stress.*
> *Step 4: The items that rate an 8, 9 or 10 are considered the big stress hitters.*

Step 5: Develop action plans to minimize or eliminate the stress of the big hitters.

PINK leaders release stress as quickly as it surfaces by developing different levels of stress relief.

If possible, remove yourself from the stress by leaving, taking a drive, or listening to your favorite music.

If it really is a stressful situation, take a walk around the mall. Retail therapy works great. Once you have calmed down, return to the office and finish your day with a clear level head.

If you are not able to leave the building, go into your office and read or listen to a five minute song.

If you cannot make it to your office, take deep calming breaths until the feeling of being stressed subsides.

All in all these methods have worked during 90% of stress related incidents. There are those moments when no matter what method you try none of them will be effective. When this occurs just submit to the stress long enough to feel your way through and work as quickly as possible to get beyond the feelings.

Stress is a part of our lives and we have to confront it head on. We need to stand firm with our tactics and move through it. You cannot allow anything to hinder your ability to be successful, especially stress.

Decreasing your level of stress will enable you to do your best.

Be Flexible

If you don't bend you will break

FLEXIBILITY IS A VITAL ASSET IN developing working relationships with others. Who really enjoys being flexible? It can be considered a sign of weakness in some organizations. Winning is viewed as more important than compromising or flexing.

Being flexible was another trait that I had to fully grasp to lead successfully. My goal was to win every battle. The victories felt good but the trail of enemies created along the way created conflict in the work environment. Not to mention the mental exhaustion that is experienced when you are in constant "fight mode."

REAL leaders are successful because they establish effective relationships. Working well with others is more important that winning. It is okay to meet in the middle. Flexible leaders are more effective leaders. It is possible to be flexible and successful.

Carry Only What You Need

※

You are better equipped when you have exactly what you need

IN THE ARMY WE WOULD GO to the field every six weeks. We had to pack our rucksacks (back packs) with uniforms and equipment. We always told the soldiers to only carry what they needed. By carrying only what they needed they would be able to handle the load for extended periods of time; because we had to carry the rucksacks during road marches and training exercises.

I would always bring extra things in my ruck to make sure that my soldiers were taken care of. I kept commenting each time that we went to the field how heavy my rucksack was. One day my platoon sergeant said, "Lieutenant Thomas, you are their leader, not their mother, you need to carry only what YOU need."

Recently, while dealing with an issue, his words came to my mind again…. "Carry only what you need." I thought about the weight of things in my mental "rucksack" and it was too much. I decided that once again, to carry only what "I" needed.

Exercise:
You may be carrying too much as well. Take the time and do an inventory of what you are carrying around. Are there things that you need to leave behind? Are

there things that you need to add? Do you need to throw some things away? Adjust the weight of your rucksack to ensure that you are carrying only what you need.

Take the advice of my platoon sergeant and only carry what you need.

Smile and Laugh Often

*Life really is meant to be enjoyed; smile frequently
and laugh often. It is great exercise*

SMILING AND LAUGHTER REALLY FILL your life with joy and happiness. Just take moments throughout the day to have fun. In Corporate America, I walk around the office singing and smiling and lifting everyone's spirits. The goal is to make everyone feel excited about coming to work. Because when people are happy, their ability to meet their potential increases.

It only takes approximately 11 muscles to smile and it takes about 72 muscles to frown. This is great information. You can live to be 100 while looking like you are 25. All you have to do is smile.

Exercise:
If you have forgotten how to smile, seek out those things that bring you joy. Watch a comedy or a sitcom; cartoons and kid shows are effective as well. Attend an event at a comedy club and really absorb the material being delivered. You can go to an arcade or host a game night in your home. Make a commitment to yourself that no matter what you experience in a negative capacity, that you will find

the joy in life that makes you feel great. Smiling and laughing are keys to a successful and joyful life.

Be Likable

You get more bees with honey,
when people like you they support you

I WAS CONDUCTING A WORKSHOP reviewing a journal article from the Harvard Business Review. The article asked the question, "Would you rather work with a competent jerk or a lovable fool?" The article discussed research that was conducted with five companies located throughout the world and in five different industries. The results showed that most often people would prefer to work with the lovable fool.

The results were a surprise. Initially it would appear that competence would rate higher than likability. Further reading of the article revealed that it is easier to accomplish tasks with someone that you enjoy working with than someone that is difficult. The creativity and innovation is derived from the positive relationship.

Establishing a likable relationship in your work environment will create a motivated work cultural that breads success. If you are a lovable fool work on your competence and if you are a competent jerk become more likable. The end result is an organization with a culture that is inclusive, diverse, motivated and effective.

Listen

❋

You can only hear when you listen

BEING AN EFFECTIVE LISTENER was not a strength for me. Years ago if you walked into my office I would continue to work and talk at the same time. There were even times when I would respond with my back to the person that was talking to me. This was so rude and disrespectful of me.

Note: When someone takes the time to tell you anything it is your responsibility to listen to them.

It was not until the feedback was given to me that I began to read books on how to listen more effectively.

There were several bad habits that I needed to resolve:

- *Did not look at the person while they were talking.*
- *Nod up and down to rush them along as they spoke.*
- *Interrupt them speaking to interject a reactionary response.*
- *Never follow up if they had questions.*

Listening skills are developed over time. When you really listen to what others have to say, you become more knowledgeable and more effective. When someone takes the time to tell you anything it is your responsibility to listen to them. Here are five simple skills that PINK Leaders utilize to listen effectively.

- *Stop what you are doing.*
- *Look at the person while they are talking.*
- *Eliminate the reactive responses.*
- *Respond only during the pauses in the conversation.*
- *Ask effective questions.*

You can only hear when you listen.

Knowledgeable

Information is power, the more you know the more you grow. Your responsibility as a leader is to be knowledgeable in your field of expertise. This will require you to consistently hone your skills and demonstrate your technical competence.

Be Technically Competent

You are the expert!

ONE OF THE KEYS TO SUCCESS is technical competence. If you are not the expert in your field, then you either need to change fields or start studying. Whatever your skill set is you need to be able to transfer that information to everyone else. You have to become so technically competent that no organization can function without your skills.

Donald Trump is an expert in real estate. Oprah Winfrey is an expert in the Media. Denzel Washington is an expert in the field of acting. Tiger Woods is an expert in golf. Warren Buffet is an expert in buying low and selling high. Bill Gates has transformed the computer software industry. All of these experts have mastered their skills and are classified as being technically competent.

Your technical competence will be derived from obtaining as much information as possible in your field. You need to constantly read, conduct research, attend workshops and training events to remain on the cutting edge in your field of expertise. You will know that you have achieved a desired level of competence when your expertise is consistently sought after over others. Your ultimate goal is to maintain your competence so that you become irreplaceable.

When you are technically competent you feel confident and you will no doubt achieve success.

Know Your Business

"I don't know" is never the final answer in business

I WAS A YOUNG SECOND Lieutenant presenting my field exercise training plan to my Battalion Commander she was a Lieutenant Colonel. It was my first time presenting information to her and I had taken two weeks to prepare. The day of the brief arrived and I was ready.

While explaining my time line and sequence of events, she asked me a question, "Lieutenant Thomas, where will the rest of your platoon be located while you are giving your squad leaders their mission." My brain just stopped freezing in place. She had derailed my train of thought. Nowhere in my practicing for the presentation did I rehearse questions. Standing there with a blank stare those three little words came out..."I don't know." It was so quiet in the room you could have heard a cotton ball drop on the carpet. She looked at me in amazement.

When the presentation was over she walked me outside and explained that it was my responsibility to know my business. She told me that during wartime, leaders did not have the liberty to not know what their platoon would be doing while they were giving out the next mission to the squad leaders. She explained that not having any answer at all meant that I had not taken the time to plan for the unexpected. If I could not tell her what my platoon was going to be doing, how could I react in the heat of the battle? By standing there afraid of her asking a simple question it was clear that with bullets flying over head I would not be prepared. She also said, "The next time you do not have an answer, ask someone who knows like the Company Commander or the Platoon Sergeant. They will know the correct answer."

In my corporate years I have found that if you don't know the answer you need to find out quickly. Knowing your business translates into understanding what is going on at all times and being proactive. After all time in money. If you are having difficulties understanding your business, find a mentor and a peer coach. Also, ask for help. It is better to ask those that know the answer than to say those three little words..."I don't know."

If You Don't Know, Then Ask

✳

The only dumb question is the one that is never asked

HOW OFTEN HAVE YOU WANTED TO ASK a question and were reluctant because you felt as though you should have known the answer? We all have been there and most times we don't ask the question. Put away the notion that you will look uniformed if you don't already know the answer. Do not feel as though your competence will be doubted by asking a question. If you want to know the answer to a question that will enable you to understand a process or become more effective then, you owe it to yourself to ask. It is much more responsible to ask a question and operate from a point of knowing than, to try and figure it out and miss the mark entirely.

Begin to ask questions, the more you ask the more you will know. PINK leaders know to ask questions when they do not know the answer.

Knowledge is powerful.

Communicate Effectively

✦ ❀ ✦

*The greatest challenge is to communicate our thoughts in a
manner that is both eloquent and easily understood*

IT IS NOT ONLY WHAT YOU say but how you say it. A wise
leader once told me, "you get more bees with honey." At
17 years old I sort of understood the message that he was
conveying but, now it is for certain that he was right.

If you are not an effective communicator then this is a
skill that you need to develop. The best method to hone
your oral communication skills is to take public speaking
courses. Join a Toastmaster's group in your area. This
public speaking forum is very effective and you will
receive live feedback to enhance your skills. What is
great about Toastmaster's are that the speeches have a
specified criteria and allow you to express yourself in a
safe environment. Another option is to sign up for a
speech course at the local university in your area. Both
options are very effective methods and will ensure that
your ability to communicate verbally will be enhanced.

Did you know that written communication is a direct
reflection of who we are? When you send a letter, an
invitation, and a birthday or thank you card and most
importantly an e-mail your words are representing you.
When writing, take the time to ensure that your present
your best. You would never walk into a meeting ill

prepared nor should you communicate in that capacity. Your ability to convey a message through words written or spoken is paramount in your path to success.

The best methodology to leverage to increase your written communication is to read and to write often. Read from multiple venues, magazines, newspapers, journals, books both fiction and non fiction. Listen to audio books as you will hear the words being pronounced correctly. You can also write blogs, use a journal, or take a creative writing course. The goal is to have a gamut of sources to leverage to ensure your written skills are well rounded.

To enhance your vocabulary, purchase a thesaurus and keep it with you at all times. It helps to have it readily available to assist you when you are writing. Thesauruses or Synonym Finders are effective tools to use when you are experiencing writer's block. It will also assist in eliminating repetitive word usage. Another option is to read great literature, Black Boy by Richard Wright, Great Expectations by Charles Dickens, and The Bluest Eye by Toni Morrison. These books are very expressive and descriptive. Finally, write letters to your family and friends this will enable you to express your feelings so that your writing becomes vivid and expressive.

PINK communication is essential; no one will ever know how grand you are until you tell them.

Reading is Fundamental

Most of the things I learned, I read

YOUR BRAIN IS THE MOST powerful information source that you have. In order to develop your expertise you will need to become well read.

Exercise:
Read/listen to at least one book a month. If you are currently reading then add more books to your current reading list. You can also capitalize off of your driving time by listening to audio books during your morning and evening commutes or while you exercise. Another option is to download audio books to your MP3 player so that they are readily available. Your brain is a sponge waiting to absorb knowledge. Reading and listening to audio books will increase your cognitive thought process as well as your vocabulary. As an added bonus you will be mentally stimulated.

Reading really is fundamental in achieving leadership success!

Focus on the Results

✣

Focus on where you are going to,
not on what you are going through

When you begin to establish your success glide path, look at the finish line, the end state. The results are what will keep you in line. As I have stated before the road to success is not easy. There are construction detours, traffic jams and even accidents, all are meant to distract you from your desired goals. On your road trip to success you will need to be able to see the forest in the midst of the trees. Staying focused on the results will guide you through to your destination.

Here is an example:

During college there were many challenges. The lack of money was always a constant concern for me. I received a small monetary allotment of $100.00 a month through my ROTC scholarship. In the early 90's this was not a lot of money. During my senior year of college a portion of the first month's allotment was needed to finish paying for text books. The combined purchase of the books and food left me with sixty five cents which, needed to last for three weeks.

After two weeks the food was running out and there was no money for laundry so I went home for the weekend. While at home the purpose was to wash clothes and eat a nourishing hot meal. I returned to school with two boxes of cereal, milk and the sixty five cents. Things were working out with only one week left to receive the next month's allotment. People often ask when I tell the story, "Why didn't you ask someone for money?" The truth was pride. My parents had sacrificed enough and asking them just did not feel right and all of my friends were broke as well.

During that month I just thought about graduating because that was the end state. Working to that end was the only thing that mattered. Nothing was going to throw me off course not even having to eat cereal for breakfast lunch and dinner. The year started off rocky but ended successfully. Staying focused paid off.

Tap into your PINK Power by looking at the end result it will help you make it through the challenging times.

Meet Your Potential

*The ultimate success is achieved when
our vision meets with our potential*

WHEN YOU LEVERAGE THESE tools as they were designed you will be successful. Never give up and know that you can do whatever you set out to accomplish.

"Hello potential! My name is…"

Bonus

Take Naps

A rested mind is a resilient mind

THINK ABOUT CHILDREN IN daycare and kindergarten, they take a nap that is scheduled daily. We often think the nap is to give the teachers a break but, it really is designed to give the children rest. We all need to indulge in naps because they are short breaks designed to allow the brain to regroup.

I constantly have multiple projects working simultaneously. In order to keep everything in perspective sufficient rest is the key to my success. Naps for me are informal rewards and recognition. They literally are scheduled on the weekends. Waking up from the naps provides a renewed energy and I am able to finish the rest of my day.

Take the time to rest. Whether it is twenty minutes or two hours, your body and mind will thank you. A rested mind works wonders.

Relax

*Relaxation reduces your stress level, chill out,
everything will be alright*

ONE COULD ARGUE THAT MY work ethic can be quantified as "tasksaholic." I will complete task after task until there are no more left and then I will create more tasks. Because of this behavior one Saturday a month is devoted to relaxing. This day in commonly referred to as "Free Saturday."

During "Free Saturday," my purpose it to let go and participate in the following activities, sleep in late, take naps, watch movies, go to the pool, have a pedicure and manicure, listen to music and eat whatever I want. The entire day, all 24 hours of it is devoted to chilling out and sheer enjoyment. On Sunday it is back to my normal regime.

"Free Saturday," provides balance and it has been a life saver for me.

When we are focused on success we feel guilty if we take a break. Those breaks are necessary or we will begin to resent the road to success. It is okay to take a break and enjoy the moment. Take the time to smell the roses. If you cannot devote a day to relax, take small pockets of time throughout your week and just treat yourself to something that you love to do. Relaxing is very effective and it works wonders.

Listen

(It's so important it's listed twice)
You can only hear when you listen

BEING AN EFFECTIVE LISTENER WAS not a strength for me. Years ago if you walked into my office I would continue to work and talk at the same time. There were even times when I would respond with my back to the person that was talking to me. This was so rude and disrespectful of me.

Note: When someone takes the time to tell you anything it is your responsibility to listen to them.

It was not until the feedback was given to me that I began to read books on how to listen more effectively.

There were several bad habits that I needed to resolve:

- *Did not look at the person while they were talking.*
- *Nod up and down to rush them along as they spoke.*
- *Interrupt them speaking to interject a reactionary response.*
- *Never follow up if they had questions.*

Listening skills are developed over time. When you really listen to what others have to say, you become more knowledgeable and more effective.

When someone takes the time to tell you anything it is your responsibility to listen to them. Here are five simple skills that PINK Leaders utilize to listen effectively.

- *Stop what you are doing.*
- *Look at the person while they are talking.*
- *Eliminate the reactive responses.*
- *Respond only during the pauses in the conversation.*
- *Ask effective questions.*

You can only hear when you listen.

Acknowledgments

· ✷ ·

SPECIAL THANKS TO MY PARENTS Mereman and Donna Howard, my sister Elle Swan, my wonderful daughter Nola Rodgers, my editor Marcella Williams and my support team in completing this book. I am most appreciative of those who were apart of the early years. Thank goodness they did not kill me. Again thank you to everyone that has been apart of the last 14 year journey. There is much excitement for what the future will bring.

About the Author

DR. DONNA THOMAS-RODGERS was born and raised in Detroit Michigan. As a child Dr. Donna did not talk very much in her early years. She used that time to take it all in. She knew that one day she would speak and she wanted to have something great to say.

Dr. Donna attended Detroit Public Schools and was awarded a ROTC scholarship to attend college. After Graduating from College, Dr. Donna served in the U.S. Army as a Military Police Officer. It was during this time that Dr. Donna discovered her passion for leadership and changing the lives of those that she led. She realized then that what she said had a great impact on those within her influence.

Dr. Donna served five and half years as a commissioned officer and then decided to change course and venture into Corporate America. She took a position with Frito-Lay in Orlando, Florida. During her time with Frito-Lay Dr. Donna has worked in every capacity of the Operations Function of the business. She has received several promotions during her career.

Dr. Donna has over 14 years of leadership experience. She is an expert in soldier, personnel, leader, employee and team development. She has lead over 1,000 soldiers and 500 employees. Dr. Donna has conducted years of research and understands the components to achieving success in any industry.

Dr. Donna has the ability to transform people and organizations. She has a realistic approach to every situation. Her style is different than most. Her methods though unconventional are very effective.

Her vision is simple: Meet your potential!

References

"*Competent Jerks, Lovable Fools*
and The formation of Social Networks."

—

By Tiziana Casciaro & Miguel Sousa Lobo
Harvard Business Review, June 2005

S.M.A.R.T. Goals and Interim Goals were derived from
Continuous Improvement Training
at Frito-Lay Incorporated

The Power Starters provide a wide range of consulting services that can be customized to fit your individual or organizational needs:

- Guest Speaking
- Leadership and Team Workshops
- Performance Coaching
- Personal and Professional Development
- Conflict Resolution

Contact Dr. Donna Thomas-Rodgers:

www.thepowerstarters.com
www.blogtalkradio.com/Ask-Doctor-Donna
email: drdonna@thepowerstarters.com

www.ingramcontent.com/pod-product-compliance
Lightning Source LLC
LaVergne TN
LVHW011350080426
835511LV00005B/229